SCRUTINEER'S
WAKE
Discovery in D.C

SCRUTINEER'S
WAKE

Discovery in D.C

JAMES GHOLSON JR.

ARPress
ILLUMINATING IDEAS
EMPOWERING VOICES

ARPress
45 Dan Road Suite 5
Canton, MA 02021

Hotline: 1(888) 821-0229
Fax: 1(508) 545-7580

Ordering Information:
Quantity sales. Special discounts are available on quantity purchases by corporations,associations, and others. For details, contact the publisher at the address above.

Printed in the United States of America.

ISBN-13:   Softcover   979-8-88514-862-7
              eBook   979-8-88514-863-4

Library of Congress Control Number: 2022911328

CONTENTS

Dedicated to the Fairmont Heights High School family: faculty, staff, students and friends.

"Orders—Answers Without Questions?"

He flicked flies, dried sweat with a handkerchief, and yanked the suspenders on his britches upward; *even with dis here heat, we built dis team to fight Johnnie—fired it in sweat. That mine be our tunnel, our underground bridge to freedom.* The thunderous cacophony caused his knees to wobble; *hands clammy, at least it ain't snowing.* Disappointed by the decision to hold them in reserve, the initial mumblings and chatter reflected an array of emotions; skepticism and frustration, anchored in trust betrayed.

He reinforced the buttons on his suspenders; he could stand a lot of things—*but I hate for my pants to slide down when I'm runnin'. That damn slap on the back of my neck squished something;* he took away his hand and examined a streak of blood—*a dead mosquito—wonder if it was Yankee or Johnnie.* With his handkerchief, he wiped both insect and blood away, re-hitched his suspenders, tightened his shoestrings, clutched the colors, USCT flag.

"Told you all that prep shit was fake—we bought it too, right down to the damn explosion!" said Grandberry. "The white man is *never* to be trusted."

Black plumes danced up ladders of smoke; sound warred with vision as the vortex separated spirit from bone. Emancipated, the inferno vulcanized tree-branches, roasted and toasted unsuspecting gray-coat sentries in a spinning burlesque.

Old man Pleasants brought hell right to the earth. Found this pistol—six-shooter; you being the color-bearer, you shore as hell gon' need it. Wafts of stench leeched to sulfur, sewer and garbage latrines, further poisoning the air. *The devil hisself is present and accounted for.*

Their practices had become more perfect; gold watches played their part, each beginning produced a more efficient end. "Faster Dorsey!" They ran: with ladders, foot bridges, hatchets and bayonets. They gained in stamina, executing as a unit, changing methods—focusing on guerrilla warfare. Low, run low to the ground, in squads of four, the best shooters crossing directions, the best runners zigzagging with the flag, all cross-training for a range of possibilities. They sang as a team.

As the morning progressed, smoked soldiers, white and black—then called colored—first into, then out-of the Crater, the whites pouring out as sooty as the Africans some of them detested. Three divisions had gone in already: *they look defeated; where is Ferrero?*

The team of African Americans called the United States Colored Troops listened, ears stretched 360 degrees, as they watched the wounded stream out of "Dat huge hole in the ground!" *Bridge to freedom or tunnel to hell?* They'd sketched, planned, rehearsed, and exercised, and made tactical alterations to achieve mastery. They'd subjected those tactics to trial and error; revision, measurement, and memorization to become a team.

"Men of the USCT 39th....Atten-shun!!!" Rapt with attention, they listened to the dialogue of gunshots, strained their mental compass to assess battle lines, topography, mind mapping nests of gunfire for Union progress. "Here we go boys—move, double-quick to that mineshaft!"A

blizzard of Minnie balls pock-mocked the rim of the dusty bowl forming their target—a foggy, smoky hash of embers, dappled blazes, angry yells, dead bodies, furious fighting by hand, rifle, cannister, and bayonet. Blood was everywhere, angels nowhere. Some vomited, some cried, most raced to fight an enemy of butternuts in a battered bowl of bog-downed blue-coats. Before that moment, they'd been rendered fallow in a theater of the absurd.

Siegfried sounded the, "*CHARGE*, go, go, go!!!" Later General Grant, commander in the east, would say, "The effort failed for want of leadership."

I

They called themselves the "Dirt Band"; elsewhere in D.C. they were called "The Unwashed," "Trepak," and "Bottoms Up." The band part was a wild association with the function of the group, mainly because the instruments consisted of a conga drum, a shovel, and a pick ax; nonetheless, the establishments and churches which featured them in services and occasional concerts dubbed them "artists."

"Dammit," the one with the shovel said, "Ain't nobody ax you to speak. Fact of the matter is you speak too much already. Don' take no h-h-hi-college degree to dig dirt, dig a hole. Anyway, we s'posed to c-c-ch— rotate on the tools in a bit—then you'll get an idea of of how damn f-f-fast you be-be- beatin' that dere drum."

"Pace, my brother—pace. When we be 'Bottoms Up' the pace be nice and slow—lovin' even; when we be 'Dirt Band,' the pace be more majestic and steady—militant, yeah militant—sos we can get the hole dug and get the hell outta here...'fore the ghosts and goblins arrive," said the conga drummer.

Locals called the place in which they were situated "Cemetery Hill," officially its name was "Ebenezer Hill," but few in the 'hood called it that. Fact was, if you called it "Ebenezer Hill," even fewer would know what you were talking about. To locals, "Cemetery Hill" funneled better into the eardrum. The sound of the pickax, a deep and ferocious bass-like thud, grounded the sweaty work and had defaulted, been missing lately, due to the man behind the tool wiping his brow. For residents living nearby, the sounds were music to which they walked, talked and perhaps even grooved.

"What happened to the bass drum? Right now all we got is conga and a scratchy shovel. I needs a pulse, a pace...whatever you want to call it. Can't be no upbeats wid out no pace...no scratch wid out no itch, no bastard wid out no bitch. Gimme a beat—I give you a scratch—shovels love to scratch, long as they have enough s- si- silence to be heard."

"Speakin' of silence, we could all stand a lil' more band and a lil less complainin':---:I got traps to check 'fore the day is done."

The Dirt Band continued digging the "exploratory" hole at the base of Ebenezer Hill as contracted by the owner of Turk's Tavern. The down payment check was signed, "Turk and Associates." It was rumored that the Hill was owned by his family and that headstones and markers in "'Nezer Hill" commemorated people in his family. The truth of that rumor had yet to be proved. Most agreed that members of his family were there, among others. Initially, the "Hill" had been populated exclusively by Caucasians, as Ebenezer Hill came into existence before the Civil War—in 1840 or thereabouts. But, others guessed that Civil War dead were there too, black, white, rebel and yankee; after all, skeletons had to be buried somewhere, and skeletons couldn't casually be identified by race.

"I can smell them ghosts and goblins—and they be sportin' fried chicken," said the drummer and he added his own flavor of upbeat to the work song being "played." "Fact of the matter is, three beers would be mighty awesome right about now...don' need six, jus' a threesome would do, a trepack. Anyways, it might be a good idea to g-g-git busy and git this hole dug...talkin' and diggin' don' mix so g-good," said the man with the shovel.

"Jus' sos you know, I was out here wid my metal detector not too long ago—one of my buds found some old coin back up near the top of dis here hill. Heard some folks the other day talking about a collar....a rusty old iron collar Turk found hereabouts...some say its been in the family for a long time."

"Old Turk used that line of thinkin' for a while—always seems to hark back to the e 'Lost Cause.' He almost lives in that period, 'cept for his taste in women..then the color of his meat changes," said the drummer.

"Will y'all *pleeease* shutup," said the one with the pick. "Why are we diggin' this hole anyway?"

Grave markers dotted the cemetery in a hodgepodge, asymmetrical style, suggesting a chaotic organization of burial plots and wide variations of activity in that same spot. Adding to the chaos, plastic bags and paper trash littered wide stretches of "The Hill's" terrain, rendering it unkempt and dissolute in appearance. High on the ridge slightly above Ebenezer Hill, there stood a lovely red barn, fronted with a large bay-window and a bullet-shaped silo which sparkled in the bright sunlight. Wide swaths of yellow sun-rays, resplendent in glorious clusters, sliced across "The Hill" joyfully emanating from the late afternoon sun. Earlier that year, the red barn had a "For Sale" sign decorating its front; now it stood without the sign and appeared to have been converted to a residence. If the sign were still there, one would not have been able to see it due to vivid shards of light bouncing brightly from the shell of the silo. If one shielded the eyes, those shards of bouncing sunlight lessened and one could follow the treks of dragonflies droning above the shallow creek separating "The Hill" and the barn.

"I can see the headlines now—'Dirt Band Finds Cannonball in Cemetery'—don't know how they gon' use it. The way folk shootin' and killin' round here, somebody might get buried in it!"

"This is D.C. proper dude; you ain't gon' finds nuttin' like cannonballs here, you got to search battlefields for that shit! Now, we got that Petersburg gig coming up soon, so bring that metal detector right along then. They want some minstrel songs too—nothing resembling Verdi or Wagner. Thats a different 'Dirt Band' gig," said the man with the pick.

"Verdi or wh-wh-Wagner—you listen to opera?"

"Listen to it—worked right down at Kennedy Center, before that, Washington National Opera...stage hand, teamster, whatever...worked all around the place; hell, I sang in Aida. You can't help but hear it. If the truth be told, opera is like being in another world—opera turns air into oxygen; it's all inclusive!"

"Bottoms Up sings Wagner—don' sound nuttin' like a toast. Man those Germans and Vikings had tons of bones all around—ham-bones, antlers, moose horns stuck in the helmets," and he sings, "Dem bones, dem bones, dem drrriiiy bones."

"Man what in the hell are you doing; are you trying to wake the dead, move the ghosts, stir the blessed spirits? You done lost what lil' mind you had. You don' know what kinda folk are buried around here— could be slaves, mad niggers, old master crackers. Somebody say you need a divining rod out here to know who's who..."

"Su-sh-shush—be quiet and s-s-s-swing that bass, I mean pick," said the man with the shovel, squinting as the sun reddened in its western descent, blurring his vision.

"Hey! Did you hear that—can't get no deeper; hit something down there dat won't move. Doesn't feel like wood, more like a brick or something...marble or granite...really hard. Bring that kerosene lamp over here, maybe I can see it a little better."

"Is it lead? Is it moving?...is it from dat other world you wuz talkin' bout. Here you go...here's the lamp; I can't come down there, bad knees—what's that you be singin'?"

"Rescue me, I need your tender charms..." sang the man in the hole, "Dats what I sings when I be pickin'."

"Man, there you go agin—must be superstitious or somethun'. Be quiet and pump that pick; shore hope you ain't split no casket. You gots to mind your manners 'round the dead, pull yourself together. Fellas is payin' us to git dis hole dug and you gon' be the one he drags around wid dat collar, unless you check yourself. Last thing you want to git out here is a brain freeze; ghost can do that to a body."

The shovel scratched the object deep in the dug hole followed by bangs of the pick. A brisk wind whistled through a line of trees lining the creek followed by a long wail. The shallow waters of the creek rippled and pooled in miniature "v's," rushing in a southeasterly direction.

A wail sounded above the rush of the wind, giving the impression that it—or something—was headed downstream. The wail carried farther as darkness grew, giving eminence to sound and impoverishment to sight; the men became more reverent in their motions, determined to "mind their manners."

"For Sale." The sign that once decorated the front yard of the renovated barn had attracted the attention of many passersby. By daylight, the barn-house made for a statuesque lodging on the inner edge of the beltway; it combined country living with access to city offices, museums, galleries, and concerts. A hundred yards away, the scene had been observed and heard by a man sitting in a tan Chevy.

Jalen Harkness sat quietly observing the antics of the three men digging on Ebenezer Hill. The red barn was a site frequently admired by him and made more poignant by the cemetery. He would sometimes drive to the site to observe the sunset reflect off the bullet-shaped silo. Though he had not heard the word "pace," the neon sign in the bay window briefly caught his attention; it spelled "Readings." Somehow the sight, with the slight chirp of creek water and crawl of sunlight brought peace to him after work. his work as a secondary school history teacher, though satisfying, often brought a degree of tension and emotional agitation. He debriefed now, down-sizing emotional jangles before heading home. Jalen and Chelsea, his wife of two years, had briefly inspected the barn as a possible home site. Chelsea appreciated the site but balked at its closeness to the cemetery, to Ebenezer Hill, so the idea faded.

Though the idea faded, the peace he gleaned from the site remained. Even at his current distance of a hundred yards away, he could hear the rhythm of the digging tools, followed by "Rescue Me," and that followed by a long wail; *somebody crying.* Occasionally, the pulse of the flickering sign and the pick would unify. He thought that coincidence of events both sad and funny; *light versus sound.* Today his job, indeed his mission at Claremont Heights had been a bit tough; he resolved to take the strange events of the day home and share them with Chelsea. The wonder of Chelsea began with her adroit capacity to tease out mental intricacies and lagoons conspired to trap the uninitiated, especially if blackness colored his or her skin. When he first brought up the idea of renovating the barn into a house and art studio she said, "Hey dude, I didn't marry you to have a big house but a big love!"

II

The sound of the evening news greeted him as he entered the bungalow they called home. Along with it came the smells of turkey chili, hot rolls, sautéed kale and hot coffee.

"Hey babe...how are you doing? From the reports on the news, you guys had a real exciting day. I got a ton of stuff done today and cooked something special—just for you! And, guess what...you better like it," said Chelsea.

"Your lips taste almost as good as they did last night Chelsea, guess that means that you still love me...nice and sugary...buns feel nice too, that 's why you fixed up these rolls—as a gentle reminder." He gave her a rolling, one-armed hug.

The kitchen was bright and warm. With her voice and chatty manner about, each of his days reminded him of his great fortune and genuine good luck in having her to come home to. When he held her in his arms now, whether it was dark or day, at home or especially away, he could intuit the contour of her body, know her scent.....*just like a little puppy.*

"It's been all over the television, that business that happened at your school. I can hardly believe that the news hounds would hunt down a story like that, but they did. Food fight in the cafeteria! One of the students videotaped some girl crashing into one of those large galvanized trash cans. Somebody sent a tape of that madness right to the news station."

The videotaped news report showed forks, spoons, and French fries sailing through the air, chased by wads of hamburger, all thrown by flailing arms nailed to the noisy accompaniment of screams and hollers. Cheers followed Tofu climbing aboard one of the long lunch tables as she prepared to launch her cannonball-like body onto a fellow coed, whose face showed uncommon fear. Crouched in expectation, the intimidated coed seemed terrified in an ape-like pantomime, frozen in ice. Teachers lunged into the panorama, yanking students away from nests of pandemonium. The entire sequence, filmed in the cafeteria of the once proud school, had happened in a matter of seconds, but in those seconds its long reputation as a gateway to maturity had been compromised. Police officers stationed at the school were seen escorting selected students out of the building. Many of the girls nearby were covered in food graffiti as a wad of ketchup whacked the lens of a smart-phone. An announcer summed up the scene.

"Today's food-fight at Claremont Heights demonstrates continuing problems at this inner city school. Remember that this is the same school where a young tenth grader was attacked last year by a female gang called the "Apôtre Chiennes" in a girls' restroom. Students have also been attacked by members and recruits into that gang on their way to and from home."

"You cannot imagine," commented Jalen, "the frustration behind the scenes at that school today. It was the first time I've seen teachers hanging their heads in disgust. A few of those kids were taken to juvenile detention; others taken to the hospital. Teachers hanging their heads; some kids crying," said Jalen. "It was seriously embarrassing—Tofu bounced on that lunch table like it was a trampoline. If you made a movie of her preps in slow motion, in the fluorescent light of the cafeteria, you could track her stutter through the air as if she were on a staircase—as if she was airlifted to that table top. Damisi slid a lunch tray it in the exact spot where she was to land. That tray took off toward the trash can like a jet taking off down a runway. The most spectacular sight wasn't even on that film clip. That girl banged into the trash can feet first, like a human cannonball. Garbage exploded out of the thing like stinky flowers. The football team sat there and watched the whole thing and never rose, never hooted or hollered, never jeered with the crowd! Coach's boys watched the whole thing with abject disgust, got up after eating, emptied their trays in the most disciplined of manners, and split for their game this afternoon."

"Oh yeah, Damisi—she's in your class isn't she?"

"Yep...straight-A student. Although she wasn't the one attacked last spring; her family really rallied around the 'Heights'; her brother or dad brings her, and others along the way, to school each and every day. Obviously, she knows how to defend herself. My guess is that Tofu was ordered by those "Apôtre Chiennes" to jump that other kid—can't bring up her name right now."

"Chiennes—what does it mean?"

"Dogs in French—or "dawgs" in contemporary lingo. Another third-world term to degrade, diminish, dehumanize. A female dog; a bitch. There might be some connection with a male gang; at least, that's what one of the officers thinks. The fellas call themselves that all the time—dawgs. Right in front of security cameras. I'd bet cash money that Tofu was still trying to make it into that gang; still trying to intimidate some young innocent, show her who's boss. Damisi's move was smooth but—you saw it, others saw it too—couldn't go without notice. Plus, it was right there on that video for the world to see; that move will come back up. The bang of Tofu into that trash can was awe-inspiring; and she lived through it—just got up, brushed herself off, and slinked away."

"I'll bet. More chili—kale? What do you think will happen now?" said Chelsea.

"Hey...your guess is as good as mine. Maybe some expulsions, maybe some charges...your guess is as good as mine. If it weren't so gross—with the news reports and all this publicity—a session or two with both of them in some sort of mediation could be in order. Principal Chambliss was fit to be tied—seems things really boil down to Damisi and Tofu at this point. Damisi is the one who embarrassed her, made her look foolish. now, it's hard to say what direction things will take. Chambliss is not one for journaling—using dialogue journals. Man oh man, this chili is wonderful. Must be your mom's recipe."

Jalen stood, approached the coffee pot, poured some coffee for Chelsea, some for himself.

"I knew you would like it," said Chelsea. "Looks to me like your school is a little on the ropes. It all sounds so unbelievable. Can you imagine anything like this happening during the time you or I were in school— jeez."

"Those days are long gone—when parents were much more in touch with what their kids were up to. Now, with the Internet and phones, it's harder to know what they're up to, help them see the traps and navigate steps into adulthood."

"So many of my kids read poorly; I remember my uncle, over in Maryland, trying to convince parents to get their kids to school," said Chelsea. "When he started, black kids were required by their folks to help in the tobacco fields picking tobacco. He was almost like a missionary traveling around to get kids in school. His big thing then was establishing a culture of beauty and a comprehensive curriculum, so that any kid could achieve success as an adult."

"A comprehensive curriculum; I read about that recently," said Jalen.

"Well, when he started in administration of schools for blacks, industrial education—essentially industrial arts—bricklaying, carpentry, that sort of thing...metalwork—those things were all considered industrial arts; the school curriculum for blacks was limited to that. He broadened the curriculum beyond those subjects. Now, with computers everywhere and present in all of those industrial activities, kids really need to learn how to read effectively. Everything is computerized now—even bricklayers, car mechanics, probably garbage workers will have to know something—read something involving computers,"said Chelsea.

"You would think that the military or educators would have recognized the challenge of reading in urban districts, rural districts too. Guess they expect black kids to have the same caliber start in life as Anglo kids... parents reading and all that shit," said Jalen.

"But that is not the case—many grandparents raising inner city kids can't read so hot either. Anyway, a comprehensive program combines the arts, academics and industrial arts...physics, English, calculus, math, history, civics, music...all of that stuff. Put it in a core curriculum to relate to everyday life. Looks like the kids themselves are headed another way."

"How did you fix this kale? This stuff is delicious."

"You like it? I'm trying to get to a place with kale where I mix it with spinach and come up with something that's tasty. I put some spinach in it, sautéed the onions first along with some red peppers and mushrooms, then added the kale and spinach...pretty good, huh?"

"Oh yeah! The kids are on the ropes, school on the ropes...hell, the administrators are on the ropes. Just saw an article on corrupt administrators...cheating with test scores, frauds in school budgets....

balling students, administrators stealing computers...it's so unbelievable. We are fortunate to have an ethical administrator...at the very least, Chambliss is a good man. By the time he got to the cafeteria, things were pretty rough; he bellows out, 'Young people, take your seats immediately!!'"

"Lot of contrast with the football team holding the reigns, maintaining their poise; things could have been the other way around."

"Yeah, but with Chambliss, you can almost predict some of the things he'll do. Some of those kids will end up being his shadow—following him around like personal slaves, being his little carbuncles, shuffling papers, running administrative errands...he'll handle it himself. He'll say something like, 'We can always use another pair of strong knees and elbows' and the kid...or kids...will mirror his activities."

"Some tough kids can think and the country will miss out on some great talent if it does not develop these kids—help them to reach their fullest potential. Black folk have always lived in this country under threat of terror; terror is nothing new to black folk. One of my theories is that this crap is happening because the kids suspect that their talent is being funked...undeveloped fully. They are just not busy or focused enough; many don't have the mental stamina to elbow their way into the marketplace, either as citizens or workers. And, many of their parents have missed the supervising boat. That's why I got out—if only momentarily. They expect teachers to control what they can't."

"So, show me some of what you've done; let me see how those sketches turned out."

"Okay—you know that statue you plan to take your class to see, the one at Thomas Circle?"

"Yeah—that's our second stop."

"Well, the sculptor that did that one, John Ward, was one of the favorites of my high school teacher. Ward had a very distinguished career and did one of my favorites, "The Freedman." Have you seen that one? I think it's in a Cincinnati museum. Anyway, I did some sketches of that one... see?" She spread the photo and her sketches out after clearing the dinner table.

"Hey—I've seen that one somewhere before—wow, your sketches are good, really good."

"Thank you. I'm going to do some more as if a light is on special sections of the body, El Greco style, then I'll render it in clay. I'm excited about it. Did you save some energy for me? I sure hope so 'cuz I'm real glad to see you. You can burn off all that frustration doing the dishes while I take a shower!"

III

"I didn't do nothing, Ma...those girls were about to gang up on me," said Tofu.

Queen Esther Turk was considered by many to be a beautiful woman; she owned things; bracelets, rings, a huge House—albeit a transfigured barn—a reasonably large bank account, a lithesome figure and a gorgeous face. It is fair to say that her entrances and exits inspired awe in the minds and actions of those with whom she graced her presence. Her husband Solomon, now retired to the land of "ex-s," was quite the opposite. The things that came to him he considered transitory. The antebellum properties, an antique barn, his large wrestler's body, his Civil war era cemetery, still prominent bank account, and hugely popular tavern were minor annoyances that fueled his great love of opera. In fact, on any early morning excursion to his place of business, one could hear grand opera being piped into the walk-in freezer that existed behind the mahogany bar. In the D.C. area, Turk's Tavern could boast a reputation which rivaled that of any east coast diner in Philly or New York.

"You cockeyed heifer, you know you are lying through your teeth. If I had more strength in my body, you wouldn't be standing on dry land with all that Potomac out there going to waste!" said Queen Esther.

Their marriage had produced one child and besides her birth had produced one other great event—their divorce. Eula Mae Turk, daughter of Esther and Solomon, was indeed the same cannonball that inspired the news reports which braved the airways of the D.C. Metropolitan area. As the child of a black mother and Caucasian father, Eula Mae...commonly known as "Tofu"...was, like both her parents, a force with which to be reckoned. Tofu had the hefty appetite of her dad and was more than prone to react to abrasive situations with her fists, than with a thoughtful consideration of consequences. Now in her years of puberty, she was considerably larger and more physical than her mother and mom found it a challenge to manage the rotund young lady as a contributing and felicitous member of her household.

In order to render her more manageable, Esther was esthetically prone to punishment of the sort that had been used to manage slaves in an earlier century. Currently, the punishments consisted of the fashionable "time-outs" that we have all come to know and love. Two old slave collars and a yoke—a pillory post—formerly Turk family heirlooms, had become hers a part of the divorce decree along with the barn house. To promote compliance, the collars were housed in a parlor and bedroom; one each. If things descended into affairs of rough-house and fist-a-cuffs, mom could find herself rendered at considerably less than peak efficiency as boss. Once this level of punishment was broached, Queen Esther had devised her own unique techniques for dealing with an equation that left her on the short end of more than one hundred and fifty pounds. The mother imagined a time would come when her property would see more concrete use.

A collar and the post were located in an anteroom situated off an escape passageway under the cemetery. Few knew of the passageway outside the immediate family. In Turk's family, the joke persisted that Mary Surratt should have built such a passageway in her country establishment. The punishment that befell Tofu upon her arrival home after the day's events at her school were of the most exacting kind.

15

"Now I got to take time from doing my readings and séances and go up to that school tomorrow mornin' first thing. I got better thangs to do other than nurse you through high school—already got you through elementary school and that should be enough to set your academic attitude. You haven't got the sense of a two by four."

Snot ran around and down the lips of the beleaguered recipient as she cried, chained to her bedpost during her "time-out." *At least, I can look out over the cemetery.* Trying to memorize the names found on markers in the quaint cemetery had become one of her favorite pastimes. *Ghosts are my friends.*

"Here, eat these chips and pork rinds for dinner. I don't feel like cooking tonight—you need to lose some weight anyhow...turn your fat ass loose in an hour, but for now you can go to hell for all I care!"

Tofu had been encircled, challenged and recruited by the "Apôtres Chiennes," but neglected to share that honor with her mom. *Got one more degree to go, one more assignment to complete, and the vote for membership might be positive—this time. If that damned Damisi hadn't pushed that tray under me. That bitch deserves a nightstick...a broomstick up her cunt and if I gits the chance...*

***

"Good morning Jalen...sorry to bother you so early in the morning. How are you?"

"Real good Mr. Chambliss, real good, and you?" said Jalen, answering the phone.

"Been better, all these events yesterday got my intestines on fire. Gas all night; wife put me outta the bed. Look, I need you to get to school early today if you can, I want to talk with you a bit before I meet with Tofu's

16

parents…or parent. I want to get your perspective on this gang business. Damisi's folks have almost put an armed guard around that girl…dad or brother bringing her every day, both in and out.

"Can you blame them?" thought Jalen in silence.

"Can't blame them at all after all that business last spring. By god, I thought these petty arguments and fights would have stopped after a long summer; guess I was wrong. I know you are doing everything you can to have these kids experience beauty, interact with history, develop strong communication skills. I truly appreciate the kind of work you are doing and think you can help me with this. Would you stop by when you get to school. Come by early?"

"Okay, I can do that; see you in a few."

"Thanks."

"Was that Primus?" Chelsea answered her own question, continuing, "He sure is up and about early today…and I have no idea what is on his mind…hee-hee."

"Yeah, he's trying to keep somebody from getting hurt. Had gas all night." *Hope that's not the case this morning.*

"It is really sick that anyone would attack another person just to join a club or gang. I mean, why not something with uplift, like solve an equation or create a work of art. It is amazing what the needs of ego will make folk do. And some kids will accept the utmost humiliation, just to be around these diseased animals."

"Hey, we accepted crap when we pledged frats and sororities. They haven't always been known for insight and wisdom, and they were started at colleges and universities. It's that group thing…need for other people. For some kids, kids without protection, it's about survival in or out of school. Shower time!"

"Don't forget my kiss!"

***

"Control or death...that was the axis common to slavery or the holocaust. In the case of slavery, death came psychologically, slowly, but it lurked large, vivid as shark's teeth or panther claws. " The words of the compact disc on the Battle of the Crater went in one ear, toyed with his brain, and decayed. He pushed the stop button; *listen to more later...surely before I head down to the Crater, down to Petersburg...if my application gets approved.*

Once parked, he thought, "Man, at school half an hour before the bell. Kinda weird to be here before feeling awake—driving half asleep." The thought teased him as he entered Claremont High, fully a half hour before the start of classes. He was convinced of the high ethical example set by Chambliss; personal sovereignty, academics, the arts...surrounded by beauty and challenged to think, critical comparisons. Gunfire had not erupted on Claremont's campus—*but it's all too common in today's schools...female gangs. Who ever heard of such a thing? Now all to the tune of gunfire and sadistic rape attempts. Might help if colleges, universities, even churches would mount reading clinics, build reading websites. Some of these kids change school four, five times a year.. The only way anybody could keep up with them is through the Internet. Where are the Marines? Can't believe how long a comprehensive, free Internet curriculum is taking to develop....starting to happen...charities and foundations abound and the free Internet high school has yet to be found. Wonder how many urban black churches have reading labs...whew man, you think too much!*

He took the long route to the office, swung by the cafeteria and made a mental snapshot of the galvanized trashcan French-kissed by Tofu.

18

In the northeast corner stood the security camera angled to capture the cafeteria floor. The garbage can was unblemished, without scar or puncture, its top firmly secured. Just yesterday freshman boys had formed teams, faking, gliding, imitating their favorite player moves— jump shots, hook shots, fade-aways and no-look passes—tossing wadded paper balls at its gaping mouth. Chambliss sat in his office with a spare coffee cup already on the desk.

"I won't say you're a sight for sore eyes. Sounds too routine, let's just say that I want to clip this...already tried nipping it, clip it down before anything else happens that brings us lousy press. Grace is trying to keep the hounds at bay; I think she's getting a little tired. It's not like she doesn't already have enough to do, reports and profiles, recruiters coming in from all over the place too since the football team is doing so well. Lemme pour you some coffee...cream? Sugar?"

"Black is good...stayed up late last night watching the news."

"Yeah...me too; Chelsea good?"

"Absolutely!"

"Look. I'm gonna chat with Tofu's folks...did I say that already?...go over the rules and regs with them. Never seen the dad at school; usually just the mom. Queen Esther Turk. Gotta say that she is a sight –for eyes sore or otherwise—ha. Just to make everything nice and legal, show them around the school, introduce them to the choir folks, phys-ed jocks, band folks...you mind if I bring them by your class or would you rather sit in here while I meet with them?"

"Well, they won't see much if they come down now. We are still in the planning stages of our tour of Civil War statues in the area; collecting fees, talking about dress and deportment. All real routine stuff—nothing out of the ordinary. How about this—why don't you call me when you need me, I'll come up and talk with her a bit about our rationale for the tour...might give them some ideas about how to bring Tofu around. I mean, she is a pretty big girl, do you think the track folks might be interested in her? She might have the makings of a terrific shot-put competitor."

"I agree...though I might dress it up a bit for Queen Esther; you got to deliver double-speak nowadays, just to keep from getting sued. Fact of the matter is, I might just get Gracie in here to record the conversation. The reporters are asking Grace if these "Apôtres Chiennes," are affiliated with "Gays Taking Over." There are so many gangs, clubs and flash mobs out there, it's hard to tell who's who."

"Okay well just call me when you need me." Jalen rose, as he placed his hand on the door, it rocked in his grip, scraped his nose, knocked the coffee cup sideways, and sprayed Primus Chambliss, principal of defacto-segregated Claremont High School, with moderately hot coffee.

"Oh, I am soooo sorry...I didn't see anyone in the outer office, so I thought you might be available. I'm Tofu's mother." A black shawl, matched black high heel pumps, black turban, black silk scarf, and an ankle length black trench-coat—the ankles glowed the same golden palomino color as the high cheek bones—greeted Jalen at the doorway. The scarf encircled a neck which flowed into ample bosom supported by a glorious physique and luminescent, glowing teeth.

"Here, have a tissue...*ancient Coca Cola bottle in motion*. This is a bit embarrassing, I shouldn't have pushed quite so hard," offered Jalen.

"No, that was all my fault."

In the doorway stood the Queen of Elegance, Dame Esther Turk.

IV

"Please have a seat Mrs. Turk; we are so happy to have you with us today. Can I get you a cup of coffee?"

"Oh no, my, my...I wouldn't want to spill yet another cup. No thank you, I had better not tangle with coffee again for a bit," said Esther.

"That was Jalen Harkness you just bumped into. He's one of our best—teaches American history. That's a tricky subject for many of our kids; for those with reading challenges, adding a subject that includes mounds of negative perceptions of African Americans, is deadly. Without a doubt, he makes history truly come alive for our students...helps them experience it as an adventure. He says making the subject dynamic—inclusion of a thing called dialectics—makes it much more vivid, more alive.

Queen Esther nodded her understanding as she sat.

"In the Civil War portion of his class, he examines the African-American response to the conflict—breaks down education, military strategy, politics, accommodation—breaks it down into a force and its counter force. Then he studies the historical tension between the two forces. I would have to let him explain it to you—not sure I got the understanding of it down."

"Sounds like some pretty involved procedures," said Esther, arranging her turban and giving a slight nod, as if to say "I see." "History must be tiring to teach—personally, I just like to keep things old-fashioned, like our people functioned during the old-days."

Chambliss flushed his thoughts fishing for a point of entry. A tactical thought came to him, *Harkness wants to do a professional development project essentially tramping Civil War sites...needs my approval...hmm, I'll approve if he buys in.* "So, we had a very nasty and vicious food-fight here yesterday, made the news and could have very seriously injured your child. How is Tofu?"

"She has seen better days, both in and out of school—but she's here today."

"Great!" bellowed Chambliss, "I hate to suspend students; the out-of-school ones cause everyone problems. Just in case you need some background information on our rules and regulations, code of conduct, that sort of thing here at Claremont, I can read those to you if you like."

"Oh no. I read quite well thank you—you do have a copy for me, do you not?"

"You may have this copy. Just covering the formalities; we all have legal aspects when dealing with the public."

"Of course," said Esther, once again adjusting her turban. "Could I trouble you for a glass of water?"

"Indeed, happy to get that for you," and he fetched a small bottle of water from a miniature refrigerator. Handing it to her, he continued, "I am going to need your help if we are to have Tofu graduate on time and be prepared for success. Remember that we had this conversation in the spring—in April, if memory serves—yes, in the spring, and we decided that you folks would work on Tofu's reading over the summer. Yes, I remember now—you and Ms. Dennison were to arrange some times, plan reading sessions for her. Dennison was to select some software and tutor her; she has some auxiliary training in reading for comprehension and speed—how *did* that work out?"

"Actually, it worked out quite well. Tofu does seem to be better, a more skillful reader. However, reading out loud can be a problem for her."

"Good...very good. Well then, I've considered transferring her—for reasons of both discipline and personal adjustment to another school. Perhaps *that* would be the best answer for her?" said Chambliss.

Queen Esther fidgeted, but said nothing.

"But before I do that, I want to run this by you. Your daughter seems to have some real issues with self-control and esteem. Now my mother was a small woman; when I'd come home from college, I would pick her up and hug her just 'cause I was so glad to see her. Now, I can't tell you how much she resented that—hated it, and said so. I had to learn to respect her wish not to be lifted, picked up; I had to respect her personal sovereignty! I had to revise, polish my self-restraint, self discipline. Small people can be *mighty* of esteem and larger folk sometimes lacking in it. You and I know that there are gangs trying to get a foothold here in the school. If it exists out there in the general society, it finds its way in here. Has she joined a gang?"

"I've thought about that and don't think so; but sometimes, I'm not sure."

"Well she can be quite volatile—you heard about that food-fight in the cafeteria. We agreed to take some steps last summer, after the judge wanted reports on her development and oversight from the school—

from us. How would you like to see us proceed moving forward?" *Forgot to get Grace in here.*

"Well, I am open to your suggestions. I would like to see her graduate from Claremont—and she does have problems, sometimes very serious, with her—how did you put that? Yes, personal sovereignty and with self-control."

"Okay, from where I sit, it appears that she is in the initiation stage, that she may have been given instructions to treat those around her as if they are passive, her slaves. Either that or she retreats and becomes very insular. Now slavery was the whole point, at least for African Americans, the whole point of the Civil War. Perhaps another class, another teacher might be able to help her see the elements and problems—the tensions of that conflict. She might relate that study to her own issues—might help her to come to terms with some of the problems she is having getting her personal discipline on track," said Chambliss.

"I see and agree; perhaps we could try that solution."

"I mean you, as an African-American woman, can imagine the frightful emotion of slave women not being in control of their own bodies, men either. Fact is, it took the Civil War to enable black men to protect themselves, to own and use guns for self-defense as military combatants."

"I would just hate to see her transferred out of this school," bleated Queen Esther.

At this point in the conversation, Chambliss picked up the phone, "Well another event like last year's restroom attempt to "Erase Virginity from the Schoolyard" is not going to happen under my watch. He shuddered as graffitti of those words, etched in orange against gray cinder-blocks, galloped behind his eyeballs. I sure hope that those Chiennes aren't after her. We have electronic surveillance all over the building—place is pretty near in lock-down," Chambliss said. Once he had his secretary Grace on the phone he spoke, "Grace, would you contact Harkness and ask him to come up here."

Queen Esther sipped on her water while they waited for Jalen to arrive. Secretly she thought; *so this is the jackass Gertrude Dennison has been telling me about.* The encroachment of silence on the conversation seemed to be welcomed by Esther Turk. After a moment or two, a soft knock came on the door. On entering the office, Jalen stated the obvious, "Grace said to go right in; we're just about to start on our Civil War portion."

"Sorry about the coffee spill," said Ester, queen-like.

"No problem. I've done that to myself a time or two."

"Jalen, thanks for coming up on such short notice. You may not know this, but the court asked us to report on Tofu when we had that incident in the girls restroom last spring. She was not involved directly; posted as a lookout or something for a handful of those *Apôtre* Chiennes. I absolutely cannot let another incident of the kind we had yesterday happen in this building. Mrs. Turk and I have had a thorough discussion about the possibilities, which include transferring Tofu to a school better equipped to handle violent students and repeat offenders. In a few minutes, I've got to call the judge who presided over that hearing and report the steps I've taken to ensure a safe environment here at Claremont. Queen Esther and I agree that Tofu needs a little 'tough love' and that you are just the teacher to provide it—but only with your agreement and approval. I have told her about the kind of tour you are planning and explained to her that you will need her fullest support. I don't want to twist your arm, but taking Tofu on would go a long way towards gaining approval for that trip that you want to make for those re-enactments—The Crater and Nashville, down in Tennessee. Are you willing to help us?"

V

From her bedroom window, Tofu had seen the conga drums beating outside the re-converted barn that night; those "Dirt Band" guys were digging a hole at the request of her dad in the cemetery. At first, she hated the repetitious sound but after a while she came to measure it against the beat of her heart. As her anger subsided, she remembered the new goal that the leader of the "Apotre Chiennes" had established for her; jump a freshman student in the cafeteria. Three members of the gang had been arrested when she failed in her lookout assignment last spring. Marlene had back-handed her jaw; *slapped me right across the face.* Queen Esther had punished her too; her mom knew there would be invasive questions and interruptions in her own routine.

"Damn Damisi," she said to herself, "gonna have to take that bitch out at some point—show her who the hell she be fuckin' wid." Being out-sized and over matched, Queen Esther planned this latest "time out" in a portion of the house which she used as an office for her palm reading and séance business.

"Now I get to look into this stupid crystal ball plus wear this damn slave collar 'round my foot. Just wait 'til I get another shot at that heifer; she don't even know her goose is cooked." She nursed the bruise that had risen on her forehead and being infected by the "Dirt Band" hummed "Rescue Me"—she hummed the Battle Hymn too, though she didn't know the words. The tunes floated her skyward as she imagined herself hovering ghostlike. She shivered a bit from the cold, shuffling her feet along with the shovel strokes coming from the outside; *can't move but one foot now.*

***

Damisi Stallworth, pride of the Stallworth clan, labored over her math assignments for the week, just after completing the computerized warm-up routine she used for effective reading. Her reading instructor had each student read a paragraph and then the instructor would read it herself, quizzing each student on the finished paragraph. "You have to read with focus and concentration—almost memorize what you have read. That way, you will know the answer to my questions without having to look at the text," the instructor said. Damisi clicked on the music icon of her favorite Rap artist, "Nappy Dawg."

"Better be careful around those "Apotre" chicks—know they will be out to get me. Didn't bank on somebody seeing me move that tray under Tofu." She turned the volume down on rap Nappy; *surprised the hell out of her butt. Just watch out for now; daddy and junior got me covered—fools always looking for payback.* "Oh well, I can't worry about that now," she said to herself, "will deal with that when the time comes." She finished her math exercises, booted-up software designed to boost her score on the ACT and smiled; "How To Best Choose Between the Two Ballpark Answers," floated across the screen. The computer program focused on choosing the correct answer, from close possibilities, on standardized tests.

***

"Jalen accepted the challenge," said Chambliss to himself, "Good. He seemed somewhat mystified that I hadn't discussed the move before springing it on him in front of Mrs. Turk. It *was* kind of a fast one—wanted to be sure that we don't end up with a another incident on school grounds—or anywhere for that matter. *Press fodder. I need someone I*

27

trust keeping a sharp eye on both of those little idiots. If either one of them were my kid, we would have a real good discussion and tune-up, just to let them understand that a little pain might exist down the road they are travelin'. Need to have a brief, pointed conversation with the girls—both of 'em. Better have Jalen in on that one." He dialed Grace, hoping she was at her post in the outer-office.

"Grace, you got a minute?"

"More than a minute," she said.

"Grace, I need to have a talk with Damisi and Tofu. Would you have them come to the office right away...thanks."

"Will do," she said.

"And have Jalen join us briefly also...it's still a minute or so before the period starts," he added.

When everyone was seated, he greeted them saying, "Damisi, Tofu, good morning. I have studied both your test scores and your transcripts. Mr. Harkness and I have decided to put Tofu in his history class. You have to do your work in that class, do your homework, mind your manners. Damisi, I have spoken with your parents on the phone; I know what they expect from you and see the evidence in your schoolwork. No pranks! Now, this fight that you guys had has been very embarrassing, not only for the school but also for your families. I expect you to maintain your academic pace—Tofu, I expect you to work on your communication skills. Now Tofu, I have spoken with your mom recently and I am sure she has conveyed to you our concerns about this group of young ruffians calling themselves "Apostles" of some sort or the other—are you a recruit? Do you know of any connection between this group and those "Gays Taking Over? Or the Dawgs?"

"No sir, don't know nuttin' about that" said Tofu.

"Good. There will be no more of this fighting between you guys; neither of you is to be servants to your emotions. Is that clearly understood?"

"Yes sir," said both girls in unison.

"I want you to apologize to one another and shake hands on our agreement. I will give each one of you the opportunity to speak in a civilized manner to the other, with Mr. Harkness here, so that we start your new relationship on a solid foundation. Now, shake hands."

The girls stared at one another warily then complied.

"Tofu, you may start."

"Well the only-ess thing I have to say is that I wish Damisi and her partners would do is stop whisperin', calling me names...'tons-of-fun' and 'cannonball.' They been calling me outside of my name—some bad ones too..."

"That's what the name Apotre means, bitch," blurted Damisi, frightened that she had almost used the word bitch twice.

"Damisi, you will have your chance," said Chambliss.

"...for more than a minute now," said Tofu "and I is sick and tired of it. I ain't done nuttin' to none of 'em." Tears started to rush down her cheeks and Chambliss offered her a tissue, noticing that the corners of her mouth quivered. "They think that they are so much—but I am going to try to do better and be a good student."

"Damisi?"

"Well, I'm sorry that I slid that tray under Tofu. I guess I was still mad about some of that stuff that happened last semester with my friend. I didn't think and I don't want to jeopardize my chances to go to college."

"You realize that Tofu could have been seriously hurt? I mean there were all kinds of greasy food under that tray...hamburger buns, creamed potatoes, ketchup—the cafeteria was just a total mess," said Chambliss.

"I know and I am sorry—I went by the cafeteria after school to help the workers clean up, but they said never mind. I just didn't think the tray would take off like that. It was the plastic that made it really scoot."

At the word "scoot," a movie rolled across Harkness' minds-eye: *a puppy dog "scooting" across a field of grass to relieve an itchy bottom.* He felt an impulse to giggle rising up in him and pinched himself to send it back to its underground cave. The thought cracked him up, given the church-like confessions in play. *Boy, Chambliss has got 'em going now. Good for him; Detroit, Atlanta, Memphis, Chicago...comic testaments to learning in black communities. Shoot-em-ups, corrupt administrators, poor learning performance, lousy parenting...git 'em bro!*

"Well then, Mr. Harkness has graciously accepted to take you, Tofu, into his class. I know how much you young students hate studying anything that has to do with slavery. But, his unit of the Civil war can help to teach you guys just how uncivil people can be to each other... and how strong your ancestors had to be...slavery gave them all the hell they could stand up under!" He glanced at the miniature "Scales of Justice" he had on his desk thinking, *I am a curriculum specialist, not a damn psychologist.*

"Slavery was one of those periods where black folk didn't have sovereignty...control...over their own bodies. But that does not mean that they didn't think...didn't debate, in their own minds and between the minds of one another, on how to deal with it. There was a wide spectrum—a wide range of ideas about why, what, when and how to deal with the whole issue of slavery. That spectrum still exists amongst black folk—you guys are living examples of it—militancy or accommodation. My responsibility is to make sure that you learn to understand both, along with respect and personal sovereignty, learn it in a safe and supportive environment. This school is a ship, a vessel bound for student excellence and success; as long as I am breathing, that is what we are aiming for here."

The girls nodded.

"Now, to help make my point, Damisi, you will shadow Grace around for two days, be her personal slave, pick up paper, make yourself generally useful, and tutor reading to special students in the classes that Mr. Harkness assigns to you. Do you understand?"

"Yes sir."

"Tofu, you are *my* personal slave for two full days. I have mail and packages that I will be sending to various teachers, errands that I will need you to do, conferences that will require you to take notes, letters that will need to be delivered, cleaning and dusting that need to happen in this office. With slavery you are told everything that you are to do; your individual thoughts do not matter. Is that understood Tofu?"

"Man. Primus is on a roll," thought Jalen.

"Yes sir," said Tofu.

"Damisi?"

"Yes sir."

"I want it clearly understood that I am disappointed by the behaviors of both of you. It is my job to ensure that each and every student gets the quality of education that helps each of them achieve adult success. You need to thank Mr. Harkness for agreeing to monitor your development; he will keep me informed on how you both are doing. We will start our shadow sessions on Monday—you may return to your classes now. Are there any questions?

Silence.

"Thank you ladies and Mr. Harkness."

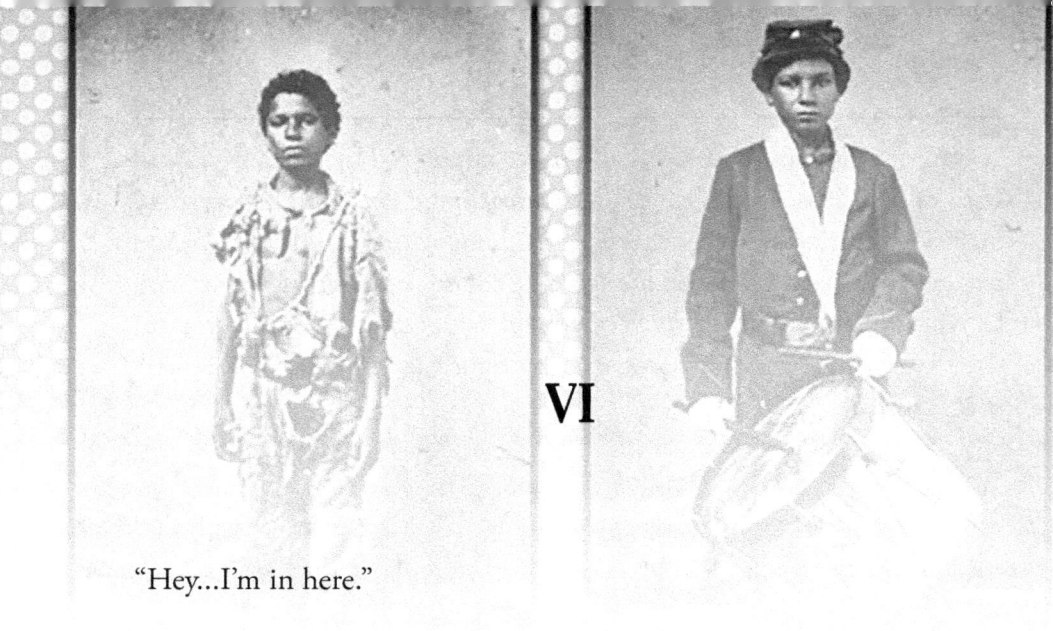

VI

"Hey...I'm in here."

"Figured as much...been all over the house, and here you are lounging in the tub."

Chelsea soaked in the over-sized, free-standing bathtub, lathered in soap and covered with soapy water. Several candles flamed brightly and sent lavender and vanilla fumes into the air; they sparkled and glittered, glowing into the modest bathroom space.

"Come on in, join me."

"You serious?"

"Absolutely. I'll let a little of this water out; I'll refresh it with some more after you get in, will wait to see the level once you get in. Get out of those clothes hon'...you shy?"

"Okay, okay...keep your groove on, I got the picture babe—hold on."

"How were your classes today—good?"

"Oh, everything went well...no hysterics."

"Your love-birds, Damisi and Tofu hanging in there?"

"Oh yeah. If all my days were like this one, the gig would be a cinch. Chambliss was in his glory this morning. Wish you could have heard him."

"Slide in baby...nice and easy, that's it. You in? Okay, now I'll run some more hot water. Where's my kiss?"

"I wanted to talk with him about putting Tofu in my class," said Jalen, kissing her at length on the lips, "...but thought better of it. Maybe it's a good decision, but I'm just not so sure. Damisi is on her way to being valedictorian of her class." He added, "She's not just a good student, but a great student. Her brother or dad escorts her to and from school everyday. After that cafeteria deal, they aren't taking any chances. I don't know exact names, but legal charges resulted from that business last spring. Apparently Tofu was a lookout, but involved incidentally. Seems like Chambliss was instructed to keep a close eye on her."

"Here, let me scrub your back—nice to have you in here with me. So you think the session went well?"

"Oh yeah, to tell you the truth, it couldn't have gone any better than it went. Damisi sent a message to Tofu directly, and indirectly to those "Apostles." Almost as good as the telegraph; messages airlifted via lunch trays: yikes. Chambliss assigned them some duty in the land of servitude. He assigned Tofu to my class—wants me to keep an eye on both of them, monitor their chemistry. Just call me Stu-mometer."

"Smart, I think that is smart," said Chelsea.

"I agree, but would rather that it weren't on my turf. Both those girls are strong-willed, though Tofu struggles as a scholar—could be her academic issues are attached to reading, or anxiety—maybe a coupling of both.

Primus attached my development leave to agreeing to take on Tofu; sneaky. Not sure I like that that; both of those kids are stubborn—in different directions. From where I sit, neither is going to give an inch."

"What do her test scores suggest. Do you see evidence of a reading problem? Now turn around and let me do your chest."

"Oh baby, you are so good to me...that feels good—could be," said Jalen.

"You've heard them read out loud?"

"Not so far. I don't want to put them under the microscope too soon. Don't want them complaining and bitching that I'm a toughie this early in the semester. I have heard some of the others reading and, to tell you honestly, some of the boys are awful, just plain awful...terrible. Calling out words with no sense of fluency—meaning, rhythm, or pulse. Okay, so your dad was a principal in Memphis and your uncle was a principal over in Maryland in the 50s. What was Memphis like for your dad back then?"

"Well, Daddy visited Uncle James in Maryland and couldn't believe the high school he had been hired at—very modern for the time. Memphis was shameful then; there was this one-room school on Presidents Island that sat on stilts for black kids—really amazingly shameful. Can some of your counselors help—help you out?"

"I don't trust 'em. That Dennison chick is a real lulu. Apparently, she was helping Tofu with her reading this summer. I get a weird vibe from her; she never really answers my questions. Maybe it's something I've done—can't put my finger on it; I just don't know what it is."

"I met her once; I don't know her as well as you, but, she did seem a little off-beat," said Chelsea. "Like she was somewhere else. Seems so many of the parents aren't in charge nowadays. I just don't see how a teacher can be in charge if the parent isn't!"

"Yeah, I agree—and that is why student achievement is not what it should be—gimme a hug."

"I'll give you a hug if you give me another kiss—maybe that's what your kids need—more hugs."

"Yeah, but none of them gits those quality hugs that I think about all day. Here let me help you dry off that wonderful body," and he brought her close to him, wrapping both in the beach towel.

"You still like my body?"

"Wrong question dear. I show you every day—well almost every day, that I adore your body."

"You don't think my boobs are getting too big."

"Let me give them the kiss test, sugar...I'll give them each a toot and deep inhales...the kiss test is always good to measure the boobs of your highness—Queen Chelsea."

"You're teasing me—better pass on that one," Chelsea said laughing. "I love puppies, but just hate those 'dawgs; way too rough. Anyway, I know you are trying, really trying, to inspire them; get excited about history, trying to help them understand the challenges of their forefathers."

"You know, once they are out of high school, many are sitting ducks for the credit market. Next thing you know, they are deep in debt. Seems like they would learn how to manage their money in all those after-school jobs they get, but that experience doesn't always translate into better money management."

"Lotta white folks caught up in that!"

"Yeah, but they haven't had slavery and Jim Crow do deal with. You look deep enough, there's money somewhere down the line. Plus, I think blacks have to develop more unique models. Stop and think about it, if the kids are not ready to deal with life after school, they live in the land of funk—anger, hostility, bad debt and poor academic or job performance follows in their wake…a wake of detritus."

"Detritus. Did you use that word in class?"

"Oh no. It rolled it out just for you honey—keeps you rolling that alto at me."

"So, you gonna tell me what it means—to you that is?"

"For my money, it means they become the waste, the garbage, debris of capitalism…fall in a whole pit of shit. If they don't think about what they are doing, read about it, analyze it, and act carefully, life turns into buying shit with their eyes. That is the trap of the capitalism jungle; it turns you into pure consumer, a consummate materialist. That's why ideas are important; they help a person think comparatively and critique the materialist glitter thrown at her—or him. I just need to get them to wonder and focus."

"Oh, I see. You've gone from 'glitter and detritus' to 'wonder and focus'. You musta caught some of what Chambliss was serving up this morning."

"Naw, it just means that I gotta rev up my traps. Poor kids don't understand that the country doesn't value a man or woman because they can breathe. I gotta figure out how to trap them into thinking; trap them into functioning from the neck up, rather than the waist down. Now you asked me about Dennison; she's a refugee from the classroom. In my opinion, she's got some issues around alcohol. Just a flat out alchie."

"That's the vibe I get. But, speaking of vibes, why don't you come over here and give me some of that banana vibe you're hiding under that towel. Gimme some waist down."

"Baby, you know that I plan to do exactly that; take you to the land of wonder and focus. You ain't said nuttin' but a whisper."

VII

"Good morning my friends—everybody have a good weekend?"

"Not bad," said one student.

"I've seen better," commented another, as assorted yeahs, nays, and mixed groans echoed throughout the group.

"We have an additional student joining us in class for the balance of the semester. Most of you already know Tofu. Let's give her a greeting and let her know she is among friends. Tofu raise your hand."

The class reacted warmly to Tofu and clapped for her.

"Now let's move on to our next unit. We'll talk a bit about how we'll handle this unit on slavery...talk about the things that are included in it and discuss the presence of African-Americans in the United States before the Civil War and during the course of that war."

"Teach...sorry, Mr. Harkness," commented Rufus in the second row, "I hate talking about slavery. Do we have to study that stuff? It's just a reminder of all the negative things people say about black folk."

Corliss in the back of the class said, "My mom and dad said their grandparents refused to talk about slavery. Said if you caught them in a good mood, they might talk about it, might say something sounding like, 'jus' git yo lessons chuld,' which meant just get your lessons child. Not only were they punished with whippings and hangings, their families or loved ones were held hostage by definition."

"They were betrayed by the movies and writers of the media, portrayed as docile and happily passive. Didn't they see those whipping posts, head yokes and collars? Musta been blind in one eye and stupid in the other!" added Camille.

"Well Corliss I expected that comment. To tell you the truth, for a long time—a very long time, I felt exactly the same way that you do. I asked myself this question, What is the point of going over all that stereotypical stuff about black folk that lasts right to this very day, about the role black folk played in slavery and their reactions to it, both in the period of slavery and during the Civil War ?"

"Amen," said Damisi, greeting the question with church-like affirmation.

"And that is what this unit is all about, really. The most important portion of that question is the word role. Because any role, any character in a role, eats, speaks, moves, acts and reacts to the conditions in which it finds itself. Is a role by definition then, dynamic or inert? Anyone?" said Harkness.

"I say dynamic," said Camille.

"Anyone else?"

"Me too, I say dynamic," added Corliss continuing, " if it were inert, it—they would be dead."

"Absolutely! And the slaves were anything but inert. More than anything, they voted with their feet and their feet reflected years of thought about how, when, where, and why they would act once a challenge rose to change their condition. My own investigations have led me to understand that there was indeed a wide variety of black thought about the conditions of slavery. Some slaves were militant, some were accommodating, some were integrationists and others were separatists. To study slavery for me was to embark on a great adventure and this adventure continues to this very moment. To study slavery was for me a study in the broad spectrum of black thought as to how to deal with an environment that was negative and unsupportive. It is a challenge to study the wake—the personal paths of thought that were taken by each slave, primarily because these paths were undocumented or sparsely documented. And for me, this is the entire adventure. *An adventurous study of the cerebral footfalls of African American slaves.* And we can find these mental footfalls in actions, in speeches, in sermons, in music, in commemorations, and in stories. Can anyone tell us why our adventure in commemorations is important?"

"What does that word mean...commemo...com—something?"

"Anybody want to tackle that definition?"

"Comes from memory...how people remember something," said an earnest voice.

"Exactly," said Harkness. "Only a dead person cannot think. If you think a person—or in this case, a slave is dead, family have a wake for that slave, for that person. Often, people would stay up all night watching the body to see if it would move, see if it would come to life. To see if that person would wake up. To be awake is to be dynamic, not static—to be dynamic, to act, to move. Our adventure is to see our forefathers as dynamic, to understand what they did and how they voted from head to toe, to see what they did with their feet. To accomplish our task, we will begin our study with a tour. Many of you, of us, have never visited sites of commemoration right here in the D.C. area. So we will begin at home!"

"You mean inspect where we live...or like a field trip?"

"A field trip to sites that commemorate events or people. We'll wrap our tour up with papers, reports, and maybe even artistic skits."

"Where?"

"Okay, good question. I have selected four sites...with one for a self study. We'll visit Harper's Ferry, the Lincoln Memorial, the Frederick Douglass Mansion, and the statue of General George Thomas at Thomas Circle. The self study site is the Civil War Memorial at 10th and Vermont. Now often, from time to time, you will see the word 'contraband.' The term suggests something illegal, like alcohol during the prohibition period. That term is used to describe slaves in the period before and during the Civil War. Slaves during that period were considered property. The 'golden rule,' was not considered a reality where persons of color were concerned. I won't get into the logic of the 'golden rule' other than to say we have daily incidents of people who do not put that rule into play."

"I know that's right," sparked across the room from a side chair, "especially with those gangs."

"Some of you," continued Harkness, "may even find that your relatives may have participated in or come from situations related to our adventure. You may be interested to know about reenactments; that's where they reenact military battles from the past. I am going to Petersburg in a week or so, to study the "Battle of the Crater." My family comes from Baltimore. I think one of my coach's distant relatives was awarded the Medal of Honor in that battle. Do we have any art students in this class?"

"That's going to be my minor," said Anthony.

"Well Anthony—and for the rest of you too—consider your reports from several points of view. Include something about your interest... if it's art, what do you think the artist or sculptor is saying about the event or person honored? What is that person doing? Where has that person been? What is that person wearing? Are the person's gestures important? Ask yourself this question, What is the aura of this person? Does she emanate grandeur, poverty...great personal sovereignty? A trial overcome? A great accomplishment? And the last question, was the artist rational or superstitious?"

"Those are great questions," said Camille, "Would you repeat them again for us...especially the one about rational and superstitious? Sometimes I wonder why folks believe the things they do...especially when they don't investigate something based on facts. They form opinions about things they never question or examine."

"Or buy something that they can't afford in their budget...if they have a budget. Or hate to study a whole era of history that they have never really questioned or examined. In some ways, it is about learning to respect the decisions their own forefathers made—or considering them dummies who chose stupidity, ignorance, and bondage. In other words, not respecting their own forefathers and, by inference, not respecting and holding *themselves* in the highest of esteem," said Marva.

"They spoke all sorts of tribal languages. That's what my mom said," added another.

"No schools to help them learn to read a new language."

"Pistols, rifles, iron chains, and whips all over the place. I like the idea of a field trip. Check out some thangs I ain't seen before...but, I still hate slavery—hate the thought that they put up wid' that sh—stuff!" volunteered Rufus.

"And betrayal if any thoughts against slavery were voiced out loud; but given the circumstances, death would have meant that none of you African Americans would exist. So the priority for them, as it should be for you, is life! And since you have life, then the next priority is to channel that life as effectively, creatively and beautifully as possible. But always remember that some brothers and sisters were complicit in slavery, both here and in Africa. You still have to analyze character, and that is difficult. With those thoughts in mind, I want our class motto to be the same as the one you learn in your religion or church house—the "golden rule. Do unto others...?" said Harkness.

"....As you would have them do unto you."

"Exactly. Now you have your questions, we have Tofu, our new class member, you know all about ties for the gentlemen, long skirts for our ladies, no gum, bring your cameras and smart-phones, pencils and note cards, tape recorders are acceptable. Tomorrow, I'll pass out two readings...one is entitled, "Of the Coming of John," by Du Bois. The other is "Cast Down Your Buckets" by Booker T. Washington."

"Do we need any money?"

"No—no extra coin; but I want you *on* your best behavior and *in* your Sunday best. Now, I've got to go to the office for a minute. You guys pass to your next class at the bell; Tofu, step this way for a moment...I want to chat with you, be sure that you are caught up in your readings. Tofu, let me know if you have any problems—either in the readings or your preps for the field trip."

"Okay, Mr. Harkness. Thanks for letting me come into the class. I'm good."

VIII

I need to check Tofu's academic profile—got her in my class now with no idea of her strengths and weaknesses. Shoulda got that information from Chambliss...see how those tutoring sessions went with Dennison. If I test her myself, it might put her under unnecessary pressure--best to check with Dennison. Jalen reflected on events thus far, turning towards the entrance of the Guidance Office before the buses would depart in an hour.

"Good morning, Mr. Harkness. Heard that Tofu had been assigned to your class. How's that working for ya?" said Counselor Dennison, twirling her keys.

"She's showing up and we are getting to know one another. Thought it might be a good idea to check in with you and get a profile on her academic skills—reading, math scores—that sort of thing. Principal Chambliss indicated that you also tutored her a bit this past summer. You probably know her better than anyone."

"Well Chambliss did *not* confer with me prior to transferring her to your class. That gang business that she was involved with last spring requires regular follow-ups from our school. Truthfully, I don't know how much I can help you."

"Anyway, I've got some questions."

"Obviously, otherwise you wouldn't be here."

Same old Dennison...crotchety—cagey "All I need to see are her test scores in reading, math..."

"I understand that Damisi is also in your class. She or one of her friends was the apparent target of a girl's gang last spring. The young lady who was Tofu's target in the cafeteria was probably selected anonymously. My understanding was that she made a comment about Tofu's being overweight or overbearing; called her out—besmirched her name— something like 'Tons-of-Fun.' Yes, to answer your question, I did tutor her a bit last summer—walked her through a reading workbook, took her some comprehension software. Took that stuff right up to her house there on Ebenezer Hill. Wouldn't say that it had much effect. Spoke with her mom—you know her dad owns that Tavern, Turk's Tavern. Anyway, I don't think anybody but me supervised or documented her sessions. You know how feeble parenting is these days."

"Last summer? Did you get some idea of how she ranks with regard to her grade level? Surely her cumulative tests reflect her academic ability."

"Okay, tell you what. Let me pull her file. I can read some of it to you— you say her test scores. Now this info falls under those privacy rights accorded students, so what I can share is quite limited given that mangy business with those Apotre Chiennes that went to court last spring."

"So what does that mean? Surely I can..."

"Read it yourself? Oh no, I could not possibly allow that, even for such a distinguished and obviously respected—at least in the eyes of *our administration*—teacher such as yourself," said Dennison.

"I appreciate your sense of appropriateness—awareness of legal concerns. The rules are kinda restrictive. But I do need to study quantifications in her file in order to develop a strategy for working with her—figure out some ways to best help her improve as a student," countered Jalen.

"It's my understanding that Primus has to file regular reports on her academic progress. Speaking of Primus, you might present your request to him for, as you say, quantifications regarding Tofu. Surely, you can't expect me to divulge the contents of her file. I mean to do that now would be risky and right now you aren't her teacher of record—ahem, at least not on the information I have. Given the legal ramifications, I'm afraid that I must *insist* that you speak to Primus. Of course—assuming you trust my evaluations of her progress—that alone should be..."

"I don't question your perceptions, but I prefer to make strategic calculations for myself."

The keys Dennison held in her hand crashed to the floor releasing a singing, lyrical ring. Jalen saw her bending to pick them up. He spotted page three of the file and found his concentration stymied and his imagination stoked thinking, "What if I just grabbed the whole file and sprinted back to my classroom with it?" Before realizing it, he saw Dennsion's feet hopelessly entangled, her torso falling backwards; the freed papers scissored the air like planes in a holding pattern or geese on a graph papered sky. Five pages in all.

Page one floated towards him; Dennison blew a torrent of wind at it, changing it's path; *cigarette smoke?* The second page barely eluded his left-handed grasp as his right hand reached for the elbow of Dennison; *jangle of tin, copper, silver?* Jalen tracked the third page with Dennison in free-fall at three o'clock, and pages four and five nudged towards a framed eagle's eye, its nictitating membrane half engaged. Page three bounced off his fingertips and lodged under a furry, brownish object. His eyes fell on a bald Dennison and froze.

"Give me that—both of them and get out," shrieked Dennison a foot from the ground, her torso firmly in Jalen's grasp.

"Of course; *yesterdays' brandy?*"

"Jalen. It sounds like you don't feel my descriptions are, as you imply, *adequate.* Let me suggest that you present your request to Principal Chambliss. When you come back with the appropriate authorizations, we can talk more about the 'quantifications' you speak of. Thanks for stopping by."

***

"Hey Grace, that coffee smells wonderful—luxury that pours!"

"Pour yourself some luxury, Jalen. Looks like you came looking for the boss, but that doesn't usually jangle your nerves. What's up?" said Grace.

"Oh, nothing like visiting the Guidance Office. Every time I visit that place I get treated like I'm a flea bitten puppy that needs to be scratched and scratched and scratched."

"Well let me ask you this. Did you get past the wig?"

"You kidding? Wigs and legalities are in full play each and everyday."

"So, what did you ask for?" asked Grace.

"Yeah, what did you ask for?" asked Chambliss.

"Morning Chief. I asked Dennison a simple question: Can I see Tofu's academic file? She wants authorization from you before I can personally examine it. I need to take a gander at Tofu's test scores. Went down to

Guidance to get that done, she sent me to you. She likes to make me jump that extra hoop."

"No problem. I'll get that for you; don't share them with anyone though, the courts have us on lockdown with that stuff."

"Great! I'm off to the tour."

"Take some pics; We can put them up in the hallway exhibits. Let parents and visitors see what we are doing around this place."

Chambliss was big on exhibits, arbor days, and general beautification. Teachers read books and formed teams to promote discussion and improvements in the curriculum. There was some resistance; one of the neophyte teachers was inspired to resign commenting, "Deed I aint gon' read *Too Late the Phalarope*. I haven't read a book since college." Music and sports were steadfast presences, with metro ratings in basketball at the highest pitch.

"Tell me again where you're planning to go," said Chambliss.

"We're headed to the Lincoln Memorial, Harpers Ferry, Frederick Douglass' Home and the statue of George Henry Thomas. They can do the African American Civil War Museum for extra credit. I appreciate your backing me, signing off on that paperwork for my Petersburg trip this year. I want to use the Battle of Nashville for my professional development *next* year; there's this black soldier—name's Moses Slaughter—that I want to check out.

"Some of the kids have stopped me in the halls, Jalen," added Chambliss. "They like you but hate the thought of having to study slavery; they think of it as degrading—the middle passage, the filth, degradation,

49

deplorable conditions and all those iron chains. Told 'em they will see D.C. through brand new glasses. I'll get some coffee for you, just sit with me for a moment, I need some too. Look, I want to apologize for not keeping you in the loop on Tofu's transfer. I just felt like I had to put her in a change of pace. I really do appreciate your taking her on. Go easy on Dennison—she has always been kinda trollish—territorial. I'll set you up with that info."

"Well for me, the new perspectives, new research on African Americans during the Civil War is fascinating. I mean in almost every nook and cranny—spyin, fighting, grave-diggin', nursing, even writing—black folk were there. I took clarinet lessons right down the street from DuPont Circle and never knew anything of the exploits of General Thomas. I really want these kids to experience that history from multiple perspectives. Tofu, too."

"Well, it will certainly give them an idea of what their forefathers were up against."

"Yeah, in some ways, many ways, that fight for Black Studies has resulted in serious reevaluation of African-American roles during that time. The National Archives has an amazing amount of material on them. Oh-oh—I've got a bus to catch—need to get going with my class; thanks for listening. I appreciate your tackling that info for me."

"No problem. Have a good time."

"Thanks for the coffee." As he passed Grace, he thought in silence— *Grace , at some point, I'd like to know the details of that legal thing that went down with Tofu last spring; the rumors are real ugly*, but said, "Cheers Grace."

"Likewise Jalen, you're always welcome. Be good and say hey to Kemo. Remember, luxury that pours."

IX

"Hey Teach," cried Anthony.

"Anthony, you all ready?"

"For the bus? Oh yeah—and I got comfortable shoes too," said Anthony and sang, "I got shoes, you got shoes, all God's chillum got shoes."

"That's good, because we have lots of walking to do. We're meeting right in front of the gym...spotted the buses there. Why don't you go on while I roundup any stragglers in the room. Take this flag; it's one like the troops used to keep their soldiers together. And you are the buddy for Damisi."

"Copy that Teach, good duty—I can do that."

"Okay young people, the buses are waiting. Everybody else is already on board. I'll take roll on the bus," cried Jalen. He shook the bus driver's hand and said, "Morning Kemo—how are you doing? Great to see you looking fit and trim."

"Tolerable Mr. Harkness, tolerable. You got 'em all dressed up and ready to go...faces bright and shoes shiny, neckties, girls lookin' ladylike. Always a pleasure to accompany Claremont folks around town."

"Tell you what—let me double check my roll. Do you mind if I take this seat right up front behind you?"

"Oh no, I'd enjoy that; give us a chance to chat."

"So tell me Kemo, you grow up in D.C.?"

"All my life man, every day the good Lord done sent—born in town, right at Freedman's, now Howard's hospital—born Washingtonian. Just to make sure, you're headed to the Lincoln Memorial first, right?"

"Yup. I want them to see that first, then afterwards, up to Thomas Circle."

"Yeah, born and *raised up* right here too, probably 'fore most of these students, even some teachers at Claremont were a just a gleam in their parents eyes. Seen a ton of students come and go, marriages work, falter, fail, and all kinds of characters callin' themselves students. Lots of these so-called parents don't know a thing about raising kids; things can get kinda rough for these kids if they don't take advantage of their school years. Seen million dollar weddings that didn't last long enough to buy a chicken wing—that's too bad when kids are involved. They are the ones that suffer, 'specially these black kids. I can predict which ones are good students, tell which ones are good with the school books." Kemo took a long drag on his tobacco-less pipe.

"I bet you can Kemo, bet you can. We talk a lot about that, although you'd have a heck of a time convincing them that this time is important. They lack the vision to see he challenges they'll face; that makes the parenting side so important; especially with all this anonymous violence. The future is never assured for anyone; its not a concrete thing you can see, taste, touch, hear or smell. For some of these kids, the wake is already in progress—the wait to see if they will *ever* be truly alive.

"Preaching to the choir, Mr. Harkness, preachin' to the choir. You know nowadays, even if the parents are together, materialism is the driver that gets 'em in trouble. They gits to shopping, gambling, buying on bad credit, trying to keep up with whomever. Throw drugs in the mix and trouble haunts the crib. Lots of 'em get compromised by bad friendships, then you got jealously, envy, control or power. Preachin' to the choir, lil' brother! There is plenty of stuff out there to trip 'em up—trip *you* up—without even mentioning racism.

"I got shoes, you got shoes...all Gods chirren got shoes, when I gets to..."

"Say, Anthony touch Tofu for a moment...she's got that her head bowed with her hood pulled up. Tell her to come up here next to me."

"Hi, Tofu."

"Hi, Mr. Harkness—Anthony said you want to speak with me."

"Yes. I want to congratulate you on the way you have blended into the class—adapted to our way of doing things."

"Oh, I'm having a good time with everything," said Tofu.

"I noticed that you have your overcoat hood over your head—is everything okay, I mean, are you feeling okay. Are you up to going on the tour today?" said Jalen.

"Oh yes...I didn't want to miss anything and especially this trip to Lincoln's Memorial. I've heard a lot about it. *Can't tell him I had that old collar around my ankle.* I'm just a little bit sleepy.. Stayed up late checking out stuff about the Memorial on the Internet. Me and my mom had a disagreement and—and, I just wanted to close my eyes for a moment or two."

"Okay...well, let me know if you are sick, keep me informed. If you feel badly during the trip, we will arrange for you to rest or take a break. Nice boots—don't forget to take good notes."

"Okay. Thanks Mr. Harkness."

Kemo lifted his eyes, spoke below the engine whirl, on the side of the corncob pipe stem. "Hey, that's the girl that was involved in that gang business last spring. What's her name, Tofu? Been to her father's place many times, out on Rhode Island Avenue. She favors him a bit, 'cept for the tan skin color—big girl huh? Does she always walk with that limp?"

"Hadn't noticed—she was transferred to my class a few days ago."

"Heard she put all of that weight on a cafeteria table, bounced off that sucker just like it was a trampoline. She's lucky she didn't kill somebody, big and muscular as she is. Bet she could chuck a shotput a mile if she worked at it! Sure would hate to have her mad at me."

"For sure. Tell me about her dad's place. You say you've been there?"

"Oh yeah—I check it out every now and then. Located right across from Cemetery Hill. Rumor has it that the red barn on the hill, Ebenezer Hill, Ebenezer Cemetery and the tavern, Turk's Tavern—were all owned by Turk's family way back, even fo' the Civil War. Old Solomon was real pissed about having to give up the barn in their divorce."

"How do you know the family?"

"One of my lady friends used to work for the old bastard—cleaning lady for the missus, cooking for the mister. Yeah, she had a ton of stories to tell about them both. Now those two, a real piece of work—both independent as hell, both had their ownliest way of doing things."

"Doesn't everybody?" *Man, sure glad dude doesn't know shit about me.* "Oh, there's Independence Avenue," said Jalen. He stood, adding, "Okay class, we're getting close, remember to collect everything you'll need to take good notes, pencils, notepad, cameras and recorders. Just so you know, I used to come here as a teenager to hear concerts. It used to be called the Watergate. All of the service bands, the Navy, Marines, Air Force and Army bands, all great musical teams—used to give wonderful *free* concerts, right at the feet of Abraham Lincoln."

"I seen pictures of that barge—right in the water at the foot of those steps," cried Corliss.

"Remember, as you frame your reports, think about the history of your theme, the perspectives of the artists and even include how you would like to have *your* own life commemorated. Think about slavery, ownership, control and property—and think—think about how individuals and groups treat property. Lastly, consider how people communicate. Better yet, do you think it is possible to *talk* with property?"

"'I got shoes'....Hey Mr. Harkness—I been singing to my shoes all morning, commemorating my *shoes*...does that count?"

"Well you can touch, see, hear your shoes, you could taste them...we split when we *smell* them...cause we probably would too. BUT, can they do the same things with you? Think about that. Can shoes sing and smell? Okay, here we are. Last thing, remember to stay with your buddy, buddies keep your eyes on the uh-uh—Claremont, this USCT flag, and stay, with, the..."

"Group!" the class chorused, smiling.

"Wow, that almost looks like part of a wedding cake."

"No kidding—my aunt had that building right on the bottom of her wedding cake—good eating too—made outa all that vanilla frosting, with white column things holding that bad boy up."

"Gather round right here young people, our guide will be with us in just a few minutes."

"I seen that Memorial once before, at night. It was all lit up and you could see it from far away, that big ole man sitting there like he was a judge or sumthin'. Didn't get a chance to look at it up close; car was moving too fast. Lemme get a snapshot on my phone."

"He sure do look like a judge, like one of them judges on television. Wonder if anybody appeared before him that did a drive-by shootin' or any of that other stuff like shoplifting, or fist-fightin', stabbing stuff, cheatin' or gamblin'..."

"Probably seen it all; bad debts, drug addiction—embezzlement."

"Em- what?"

"You know—embezzlement, stealing from the boss."

"Good morning boys and girls. It's great to have you here with us this morning at the Lincoln Memorial. The Lincoln Memorial was dedicated in 1922. It is surrounded by thirty-six Greek style Doric columns, which is the same number of states in the Union at the time of Lincoln's death. You can see the names of the states at the very top of the building's structure. Let's get a little closer, so you can get a good look at the statue. Be sure to tie those shoestrings so you don't trip young lady," said the tour guide, "you might want to lean on your buddy; you seem to be limping a bit."

"Yes, ma'am," said Tofu.

"Lincoln was noted for his ability to listen and find a suitable metaphor, be it a joke or a morality tale. The ability to listen, rephrase what he had heard, and flip the coin—create the other side of an argument brought about trust in his listeners. That is why the sculptor has him seated as if on a judge's bench—in a position of trust. Roman architecture considered statues seated in this manner as a means of assigning its honoree perpetual greatness. Two different people participated in the development of this Memorial; they were Henry Bacon, architect, and sculptor Daniel Chester French."

"As we get closer to the sculpture, I want you to think about mood; what mood of Lincoln's do you think the sculptor was trying to capture? As you know already, slavery of African Americans was the law of the land in the south before the Civil War. Discussions, debates and then violence erupted as abolitionist John Brown threatened violence against slave masters and slave laws. As a thirty-six state nation of laws, there was profound ethical—moral, disagreement regarding the basic humanism of slaves. As a result, slaves were labeled as 'contraband' or 'thinking property.' In a sovereign country, secession is the same as divorce between married people. This conflict in culture, between the industrial north and agrarian south—the southern agrarian states depended upon slaves to work the land—resulted in the American Civil War, which for many citizens was about preserving the Union. In order to save the Union, it became increasingly pragmatic to not only free the slaves, but to engage slaves in the military effort as active combatants, spies, teamsters, cooks, and seamstresses. Are there questions so far?"

"Did they make the sculpture here—outside?"

"Oh no, Mr. French had a home studio in Stockbridge, Massachusetts. He did three plaster models before selecting the model for the final colossus—the final statue which you see here, to be made out of marble. The design process for the artistic enterprise of creating a statue is quite involved. In general, it requires many steps, planned in accordance with the nature of the materials and the artistic vision. Most sculptors prepare sketches, study pieces, clay models, photos, and several *plaster* models to assist, to help them achieve their vision, their final product."

"So is this statue of Lincoln sculpted by hand?"

"Good question, once French was satisfied with his final plaster design, his final piece was prepared and carved—by hand, from Georgia marble. Legend has it that if you are very, very quiet and listen to the wind, you can hear the marble speak, hear Lincoln delivering the Gettysburg address. Now I have listened quietly on occasion and haven't been quite so lucky—I have tried that. On those occasions where I was exceptionally quiet and closed my eyes, I could hear feet moving up the long set of steps leading to the Memorial—some barefoot and some with shoes. During those times, when I heard footfalls, they blended in with the sound of water in the Reflecting Pool and I thought I could almost hear that voice. But I always heard the feet first!"

"I think I can hear a voice...high and thin...coming from up behind that cloud," whispered Conrad in a voice modulated so that only Spence could hear.

"You should record it then. I'm going to record the feet—the footfalls. If you close your eyes and focus, the sound of the different feet and shoes cries in grunts and groans—like a stomach crying 'feed me.' See, if I put my cassette recorder right on this cold floor, I can get me a good recording," teased Spence.

"You gonna get a zillion shoes scratchin', but none of them gon' sound barefoot like the slaves she was talkin' about. Ain't gonna get nothin' but a drummin' and scratchin' of shoes."

"Maybe—but I betcha, hey look—right down there—somebody lost their sunglasses. Tofu—can you reach 'em, right behind that bush, pretend like you dropped something and go get 'em."

"I can't. I hurt my leg!" retorted Tofu, her voice dialed low. "You do it—Anthony's waving that flag, you ain't doing nothin' but runnin' yo mouth."

"Anymore questions? If not, I want to let you know that I have enjoyed my time with you. I can take some pictures if you like. There is an acoustical trick available to you. If you stand in this corner and whisper, another person standing over there in that corner can hear you quite clearly. Can even hear boys talking about *sunglasses*. If you have more questions, feel free to email me. I will give my card with my email address to your teacher. Please enjoy your visit to the Lincoln Memorial," said the guide.

"Okay—but walk slow, so I can catch up with the group," said Spence.

"Run and stop gabbin'," said Tofu.

"Spence, what are you doing?" said Jalen.

"Dropped some shades, Teach. Had to run down and get them; see?" He held up the sunglasses. "I was watching all those feet, marchin', first down the steps and then while I was comin' back up—almost like a *mountain* of feet rollin' up those steps when you look at 'em from the bottom."

"Okay. Well catch up with Tony and Damisi, up by that USCT flag. Kemo, I think we are just about ready to go, to head up to see General Thomas in all his glory."

"Yo, I'll rev her up. Watch Tofu as she comes down those stairs. She been limping all morning."

"Will do—don't want any accidents, wouldn't be good for business."

"Hey Mr. Harkness. Tofu thought that these were some sun-glasses that she lost, but they are way too big for her. She wants me to give them to you," said Spence.

"Thank you Spence—I'll keep them in a safe place. You get some pictures of President Lincoln?"

"Oh yeah. I read that Gettysburg Address too; it's kinda short."

"Yep. They said that when Lincoln delivered it also; short enough for you to memorize if you don't pay better attention. Class! It's time to board the bus."

X

"Wow, that almost looks like part of a wedding cake."

"No kidding—my aunt had that building right on the bottom of her wedding cake—good eating too—made outa all that vanilla frosting, with white column things holding that bad boy up."

"Gather round right here young people, our guide will be with us in just a few minutes."

"I seen that Memorial once before, at night. It was all lit up and you could see it from far away, that big ole man sitting there like he was a judge or sumthin'. Didn't get a chance to look at it up close; car was moving too fast. Lemme get a snapshot on my phone."

"He sure do look like a judge, like one of them judges on television. Wonder if anybody appeared before him that did a drive-by shootin' or any of that other stuff like shoplifting, or fist-fightin', stabbing stuff, cheatin' or gamblin'…"

"Probably seen it all; bad debts, drug addiction—embezzlement."

"Em- what?"

"You know—embezzlement, stealing from the boss."

"Good morning boys and girls. It's great to have you here with us this morning at the Lincoln Memorial. The Lincoln Memorial was dedicated in 1922. It is surrounded by thirty-six Greek style Doric columns, which is the same number of states in the Union at the time of Lincoln's death. You can see the names of the states at the very top of the building's structure. Let's get a little closer, so you can get a good look at the statue. Be sure to tie those shoestrings so you don't trip young lady," said the tour guide, "you might want to lean on your buddy; you seem to be limping a bit."

"Yes, ma'am," said Tofu.

"Lincoln was noted for his ability to listen and find a suitable metaphor, be it a joke or a morality tale. The ability to listen, rephrase what he had heard, and flip the coin—create the other side of an argument brought about trust in his listeners. That is why the sculptor has him seated as if on a judge's bench—in a position of trust. Roman architecture considered statues seated in this manner as a means of assigning its honoree perpetual greatness. Two different people participated in the development of this Memorial; they were Henry Bacon, architect, and sculptor Daniel Chester French."

"As we get closer to the sculpture, I want you to think about mood; what mood of Lincoln's do you think the sculptor was trying to capture? As you know already, slavery of African Americans was the law of the land in the south before the Civil War. Discussions, debates and then violence erupted as abolitionist John Brown threatened violence against slave masters and slave laws. As a thirty-six state nation of laws, there was profound ethical—moral, disagreement regarding the basic humanism of slaves. As a result, slaves were labeled as 'contraband' or 'thinking property.' In a sovereign country, secession is the same as divorce between married people. This conflict in culture, between the industrial north and agrarian south—the southern agrarian states depended upon slaves to work the land—resulted in the American Civil War, which for many citizens was about preserving the Union. In order to save the Union, it became increasingly pragmatic to not only free the slaves, but to engage slaves in the military effort as active combatants, spies, teamsters, cooks, and seamstresses. Are there questions so far?"

"Did they make the sculpture here—outside?"

"Oh no, Mr. French had a home studio in Stockbridge, Massachusetts. He did three plaster models before selecting the model for the final colossus—the final statue which you see here, to be made out of marble. The design process for the artistic enterprise of creating a statue is quite involved. In general, it requires many steps, planned in accordance with the nature of the materials and the artistic vision. Most sculptors prepare sketches, study pieces, clay models, photos, and several *plaster* models to assist, to help them achieve their vision, their final product."

"So is this statue of Lincoln sculpted by hand?"

"Good question, once French was satisfied with his final plaster design, his final piece was prepared and carved—by hand, from Georgia marble. Legend has it that if you are very, very quiet and listen to the wind, you can hear the marble speak, hear Lincoln delivering the Gettysburg address. Now I have listened quietly on occasion and haven't been quite so lucky—I have tried that. On those occasions where I was exceptionally quiet and closed my eyes, I could hear feet moving up the long set of steps leading to the Memorial—some barefoot and some with shoes. During those times, when I heard footfalls, they blended in with the sound of water in the Reflecting Pool and I thought I could almost hear that voice. But I always heard the feet first!"

"I think I can hear a voice...high and thin...coming from up behind that cloud," whispered Conrad in a voice modulated so that only Spence could hear.

"You should record it then. I'm going to record the feet—the footfalls. If you close your eyes and focus, the sound of the different feet and shoes cries in grunts and groans—like a stomach crying 'feed me.' See, if I put my cassette recorder right on this cold floor, I can get me a good recording," teased Spence.

"You gonna get a zillion shoes scratchin', but none of them gon' sound barefoot like the slaves she was talkin' about. Ain't gonna get nothin' but a drummin' and scratchin' of shoes."

"Maybe—but I betcha, hey look—right down there—somebody lost their sunglasses. Tofu—can you reach 'em, right behind that bush, pretend like you dropped something and go get 'em. "

"I can't. I hurt my leg!" retorted Tofu, her voice dialed low. *You* do it—Anthony's waving that flag, you ain't doing nothin' but runnin' yo mouth."

"Anymore questions? If not, I want to let you know that I have enjoyed my time with you. I can take some pictures if you like. There is an acoustical trick available to you. If you stand in this corner and whisper, another person standing over there in that corner can hear you quite clearly. Can even hear boys talking about *sunglasses*. If you have more questions, feel free to email me. I will give my card with my email address to your teacher. Please enjoy your visit to the Lincoln Memorial," said the guide.

"Okay—but walk slow, so I can catch up with the group," said Spence.

"Run and stop gabbin'," said Tofu.

"Spence, what are you doing?" said Jalen.

"Dropped some shades, Teach. Had to run down and get them; see?" He held up the sunglasses. "I was watching all those feet, marchin', first down the steps and then while I was comin' back up—almost like a *mountain* of feet rollin' up those steps when you look at 'em from the bottom."

"Okay. Well catch up with Tony and Damisi, up by that USCT flag. Kemo, I think we are just about ready to go, to head up to see General Thomas in all his glory."

"Yo, I'll rev her up. Watch Tofu as she comes down those stairs. She been limping all morning."

"Will do—don't want any accidents, wouldn't be good for business."

"Hey Mr. Harkness. Tofu thought that these were some sun-glasses that she lost, but they are way too big for her. She wants me to give them to you," said Spence.

"Thank you Spence—I'll keep them in a safe place. You get some pictures of President Lincoln?"

"Oh yeah. I read that Gettysburg Address too; it's kinda short."

"Yep. They said that when Lincoln delivered it also; short enough for you to memorize if you don't pay better attention. Class! It's time to board the bus."

XI

"Kemo, let's hit DuPont Circle going up Connecticut Avenue—might be a little quicker if we angle in; hopefully we'll have at least an hour at Thomas Circle. I'll call that burger joint, tell em we're on the way so as not to hit them with a twenty-four-body surprise."

"Sounds like a winner...should be pretty fast going up that way, except for the delivery trucks. That Park Service guide was good. Always impressed by the training that they impart on those guides," said Kemo.

"You know, I used to take clarinet lessons right there at DuPont Circle—right at eight o'clock on the southwest side. Used to see Italian girls in long sleeve white blouses, white dudes all suited up with attache cases. Every now and then a black dude driving a delivery truck. All that's changed."

"That was part of an inter-continental vision; Lincoln had started to see it, though his vision was hazy. Douglass saw it bright and clear. Put black folk in the game, whatever it took to make the footing equal. Sounds a little clichéd now, but it still takes fortitude of heart and mind to get these kids where they are ready mentally—physically too. That control demon, the agent of hierarchies, still running rampant in the good ole' U.S. of A. Every now and den I watch those fights of Muhammad Ali to get my juice up 'cause somewhere down the line, I *know* a fights comin'."

"You're right about Douglass...way ahead of his time. These little egos gonna get some bruising and crushing along the way; they don't see it coming mostly. Think the playing field is level."

"That's why you got 'em out here. There's the joint right over there."

"Okay young people—Mr. Chambliss gave us monies from the slush fund to do lunch—you have forty-five minutes for lunch. Let's sync up, set your watches—I have eleven-thirty. You are due back here at 12:15 sharp. We will stay together. If you don't have a watch, stay in a group that has one. If you get lost, we re headed down Massachusetts Avenue two blocks to Thomas Circle. Best thing is to keep your eyes looking out for the 13th USCT flag right here. Stay with the group! Find the flag or call me on my phone if there's a problem; stay with your buddy at all times."

"Hey—I see a parking spot...hold on. Let's park first, then I can help you with your students."

"Good idea...I'll get out and help guide you in...all these druggies and prostitutes...totally different from when I was a kid. Look at those folks over there."

"Hey Needles...Needles Harkness!!"

I hear my nickname...but nobody out here knows that nickname...none of my students
knows anything about Needles. That's my—my high-school nickname.

"Needles. Jalen Harkness."

 "I've heard that voice before. I know that voice," thought Jalen.

"It's coming from over there Jalen...that person. I think it's that voice over there, over there in that getup. She's waving at you. Uh, she acts like she knows you."

Jalen had almost spun a 360 when he spotted the waving arm. "I don't see where you are...oh—oh yeah, I see."

"You good?" questioned Kemo.
"

"Oh yeah, I got this Kemo—get the kids off the bus if you don't mind, and walk them up to the restaurant. This chick knows me from somewhere; I'm gonna stay here and talk with her for a moment."

"Okay, okay...Let's go people...we're on a time-line," barked Kemo; he shot Jalen a cockeyed grin, fried in a greasy backspin. "You be careful now."

"Man, it's been a month of Sundays since I've seen you—haven't seen you since graduation time. You don't—hey, not to be puzzled bro. Don't judge the book by it's cover, man I forgot, I 'm on observation detail in Dupont Circle. Royce, from back in the day."

"Royce, Royce Rice. But—what's with the getup—I would never?"

"I'll tell you all about that—what are you doing out here?"

"Damn man...Royce, why the hell are you all dressed up like that? You got on that dress, high heels—big-ass purse. I thought you were one of those pigeon feeders, a gay bum getting jacked up or peddlin' pussy—a prostitute, transvestite—or damn man, or—something. Geez, you say you are doing what?"

"Ha-ha—embarrassed you huh," said Royce cracking up. "FBI/DC squad; kinda an undercover, observation detail bro, keepin' crime at bay, off balance, patrol the Circle for depraved-heart shenanigans brother. You didn't recognize me did you? Probably shouldn't have called you, but man, I haven't seen you since high school. What are you doing out here?"

"I teach—up at Claremont. Been teaching up there for eight, nine years. Wanted to bring my kids to various sites around town, statues and memorials—stuff that commemorates the Civil War. Most of them have never seen this stuff. With all this weird bull rollin' in D.C. these days, I'm trying to find ways to boost their sense of personal dignity. Damn! Royce Rice with a do-rag, dress, big purse—shit man, coach would be amazed! We're headed to Thomas Circle. You know, I was out by the school the other day....riding out by the old hood. Remembered how we used to sing do-wops after basketball practice, walkin' and singing in snow and hail, right down Addison Road—oh mein, those were the days. Look, here's my card. Call me, let's get together, talk about old times. Deal?"

"You bet—will do—you married?" said Royce.

"Long conversation Jalen. Be good my man, great to see ya—call me and take care. You—you do that married thang?"

"Yep—I'll bring her," said Jalen.

"Great! I'd like that."

Damnation—Royce Rice! Now I've seen it all.

"Kemo. Let me grab a sandwich; I'll eat and move. Let's go people, time to move it! A little about Thomas Circle while we travel."

Jalen stood facing the students near the front of the bus. "The bronze statue of General George Thomas was dedicated on Nov. 19, 1879. The statue was designed by John Quincy Adams Ward. The pedestal on which it sits was designed by J.L. Smithmeyer. Ward was commissioned—that means paid—by the Society of the Army of the Cumberland to create this naturalistic sculpture of the 'Sledge of Nashville.' Ward had already sculpted a wonderful work called "The Freedman." Thomas is astride his horse on a slight incline and the sculpture is considered to be the finest example of equestrian statues in our 'Nation's Capitol.' To my mind, General Thomas is the finest general of the Civil War; he was both strategic and a tactical genius and never suffered a defeat in any of his campaigns. Plus, he was fair-minded and always thoroughly prepared.

"We'll stay on the bus. Kemo will engage, hug the roundabout for a couple of times very slowly so you folks can take pictures. General Thomas was the first Union General to purposely design a role for African American soldiers at the Battle of Nashville. I am headed to Petersburg in a few weeks to re-enact the Battle of the Crater; *look for the footfalls of Decater Dorsey.* My flag that we are using as a rally point, honors the 13th USCT, the regiment of African-American soldiers at Nashville. General Thomas and his sisters narrowly escaped the rebellion of Nat Turner in Virginia, when he was a child. They were so pissed with him for keeping his oath to the Union that they would never speak to him again. He was beloved by the soldiers under his command and they especially fought hard for a commander who interacted with them on an analytical level. His gift for gaining strategic intelligence from black slaves was practically unparalleled."

"I can't tell you a lot about how the statue was made—but do note the gestures of General Thomas and his horse, Billy. The horse's mane and tail wave bravely in a brisk wind, his ears perked for signs of battle, with Thomas facing southward as if listening for various intonations—light arms, artillery or battery—of the battle. General Thomas is best known for his stand at Chickamauga; if you ever get to see Chickamauga, don't miss it! After that battle, he was nicknamed 'The Rock of Chickamauga.' The statue is a supreme example of artistic modeling and accuracy of features and proportion. The same sense of beauty, accuracy and naturalism can be seen in his sculpture of 'The Freedman,' which shows a near naked former slave with shackles recently burst."

"Was that somebody that you knew back there?"

"An old friend—someone near and dear to me when I was about your age. We roamed DC together, rummaging for basketball competition."

Kemo grunted an "Ahem," clearing his throat, "choked on pipe-smoke."

"Any questions about General Thomas? Everybody got photos, notes—both? Then wave to the General and we will head back to school."

"Uuggh."

XII

"This chair needs height, it's way too low," said Tofu, fantasizing while she sat on the French high-back chair. "It don't wobble, but needs more elevation; more height means more importance. Strange and weird," she thought to herself, confused by the exhilaration, the kernel of ecstasy she'd felt from the speed of her body careening toward a trash can; *weird, almost magic.* Pain had come, bruises lingered, but the thrill of the hurtle, the speed, remained outweighing the throb in her ankle.

"I gotta get the feel of this fast, she might return anytime." Tofu, comfortably seated in the chair of modest height, genuflected towards the crystal ball centered on the table in the séance bunker. The glass oval, massive in density and eight inches tall, threw reflections to her eyes of wizened jaws and chunky cheeks, elongated fingers, and piggish eyes. Upon weight testing its mass, below the smooth surface, she winced. Puzzled, she hummed a long lyrical melisma, one ear cocked towards the door, her nerves at high alert. Queen Esther had gone grocery shopping. Violation of the sanctity of the séance parlor had consequences. "I need a chair like Lincoln's—with thousands of slaves—by a pool."

Made confident by the soft whirl of the outdoor chimes, she floated, buoyed by the echoed sound of conga drums. The memory of chains around her ankle diminished her euphoria. Mom applied an archaic punishment, the same she herself had received as a child, to her daughter as a kind of "time out" in the ancient slave style—a fossil of southern purgatory. Tofu reminisced on the Reflecting Pool across from Lincoln's Memorial, briefly considering her sobering crash into the trash can.

"Did you lose your brains before you jumped or after you hit the trash can? Did you gain some brownie points with whomever you were trying to impress by flying on a lunch tray?" Those were the questions mother Queen Esther had tossed her way. "And look at all those stupid bruises you have on your body. A few more from that slave collar around your ankle won't make one bit of difference." Tofu reflected once more on the ill-advised jump she had made to coerce obedience from a wide-eyed Constance.

"Jumped too high. Shoulda grabbed that silly bitch; grabbed her and put a elbow lock on her tired butt. Forgot all about that damned Damisi." In her mind, she envisioned the lunch tray as a magic carpet rising high above the statue on Thomas Circle. *If I get the hang of this sunlit cruise, I can rise above whatever gets in my way.* One of her big sisters had said, "Silly coquette, fat hussy—you gone and done it now, gone and showed de whole world that you is recruiting slaves—out there hustling for peons and attention."

The bruise on her ankle, still somewhat swollen, felt inconsequential; the bone underneath it, the place where her mother clamped the foot collar, was tender and throbbed. *Damn foot collar.* She touched her ankle gingerly. She felt her ears twitch. *Yeah, I need one of those large Lincoln chairs, a big ole stallion to ride, a tray for my magic carpet, and tons of umbrellas collected poolside for the slaves.* What surprised her was the thrill she'd felt right along with all that embarrassment.

A red flame flickered above the candle she had lit in her effort to recreate the aura of a séance, which in truth she had yet to witness in the flesh. "No matter," she thought, "even if I ain't seen the real thing, I know what I need to get the ball rollin'." She surveyed the room for its essential ingredients: *a wooden round table, a clear crystal ball, several high back chairs, sum candles, and one of dem yokes...stocks thing... like that one in the corner of the bunker.* From outside the room, she heard another whirl of the chimes flare; it had repeated that same tune when the gravediggers bolted in disbelief. Something down there had frightened them. *Maybe it was my trick; was that why that hole was left open for days? Spooky!"*

Tofu blew a sustained column of air at the flame to test its durability; the oscillations surged. "I need all this stuff in my kingdom, once I gits my chair and horse. Won't nobody have nuttin' on me den, bet I'll get me more confidence, be a better student too," she thought, "be just as good as anybody, green, blue, yella or white, maybe admired; *famous.* Ain't nebba seen no statue of a woman in D.C. Not that I seen 'em all. One thing for sure, even those Apostle bitches...Apôtre Chiennes... better start talking to me in a different style; I sure don't plan on making a habit of French-kissing trash cans."

"Get your game on bitch," that's what big sister had screamed at her on the phone. "Your game on, your coquette ass in gear, and get it...done! Put the skeer on 'em, skeer that *esteem* shit right out of 'em." *Everybody usin' that word esteem, gotta see what it mean.*

"Get your game on, get it...done!" Her own voice surprised—frightened her now as she yelled authoritatively, "Comb my hair, run my water, fetch my d..dr....pants!" *Queens live in big houses, not damn red barns. Momma likes barns, Dennison likes barns. Damn Dennison said she would help bring out the best in me, said she would help me with my academics... ended up in a bunker party! Heiffer! Her and momma seancing 'til the wee, wee hours.*

From outside, the whine of a car engine broke the chirp of chimes, arrested her muse. In a flash, she blew out the candle, fanned the air to disperse the aroma of vanilla, and scurried up the stairs. To Tofu, the whirl of the outdoor chimes simulated the same tune the gravediggers sang; *done mastered that tune with my hoots and whistles.*

***

Jalen's heart purred like a kitten at weeks' end; it had little, really nothing, to do with Friday. The purr had the tempo and rhythm of "shoo-dooby, shooby-doo." The sound and rhythm ghosted him all week; a happy haunting echo of his high school years. Those joyful years kept defeatism at bay: *shoo-dooby, shooby-doo; yeah!"* They had harmonized, improvised, and proselytized those words up and down the byways of Sheriff Road, Addison Road, and Kenilworth Avenue seeking out competition on the basketball courts of northeastern D.C. The melody was one of those that stuck with him in tune, tempo, and its 50's harmony: *easy to recall, no modulation at the bridge.* By the time the weekend had arrived, the countless repetitions ground the tune to dust, even drowning out thoughts of his upcoming Petersburg trip. Royce loved to sing the lead melody and led with a reasonably big voice. Occasionally, they were joined by some of the bigger guys on the team, with really high falsetto-capable voices; just another proof of what a freezing, windy, cold and snowy night can do.

"Chelsea," he said pouring her an after dinner beer and himself a vodka Collins, "you will not believe what happened to me on our little school tour."

"If I promise I will believe you, does that mean you'll do the dishes?"

"Hey baby, if that what it takes for you to listen, you're on. I will do them anyway, but listen to my story—you're the only person who can truly appreciate it."

"I am your devoted audience, lock, stock, and barrel. Tell me your story."

"Okay. So we're at the Lincoln Memorial, heading up Connecticut to DuPont Circle—headed that way to get lunch before going to see

General Thomas at Thomas Circle—you know, right there at 10th and Vermont. Kemo, our bus driver, is doing a masterful job of navigating traffic, and not only do we get to DuPont Circle in record time, we also find a parking space nearby. So, we're are about getting the kids some lunch—I get off the bus, and I hear this voice calling my name but I don't see anybody I know—looked all around. All of a sudden, Kemo points out this chick...had on a bright do-rag, high- heels, *a saddlebag* for a purse!"

"Like mine?"

"Yours is dainty compared to this. And this, this...individual, this person is waving at me and calling me by name. Jeez! All the kids looking back, giggling, chortling and shit. So the voice is high-pitched, but that of a dude, the body has the trappings of dude-ism—the clothes are *strictly* female. I stop, we talk—it's Royce Rice! Remember me telling you about this guy on the school basketball team? Had the most gorgeous floater you ever saw for a right-handed shooter moving to the left. Vicious too! That bad boy would knife the back of the rim like a dagger to the heart."

"Sounds like he might have changed a bit since the last time you saw him."

"Changed? I was completely dumbfounded 'til he was about yea close. We used to sing du-wops constantly. Shoo-dooby, shooby-doo. Fact is, one of those du-wops has been with me all day, actually all week."

"I know—a cautionary song."

"Anyway, we get to talking. Turns out, he's in the detectives and doing some undercover stuff—requires him to do this getup. None of the kids *said* anything, but I know they were wondering. Man, their eyes were about to pop all the way out."

"I want you to sing it again for me—but not now, later. So did you get his number?"

"I did. Lemme see, oh and we found these old sunglasses too. I'll keep them in this jacket for Petersburg. Anyway, I got his card, got his telephone number and we talked about doing dinner soon. I can't begin to count the number of times we sang, 'In the Still, shoo-dooby, shooby-doooo, of the Ni-ight' coming home from basketball practices. Royce Rice with *transparent,* high-heel slippers—good grief. We have got to do dinner soon; I want you to meet him."

"Sounds like a plan. So how did the tour go?"

"The kids got tons of pictures, sketches—some of them had seen the Reflecting Pool, but not the Memorial up close. Fact is, that pool is a huge incentive to think, contemplate, seriously develop reflective thinking for a lifetime, a metaphor for lifelong learning."

"That's another reason I love you hon'. Keep 'em excited about what you've got planned. Nowadays, kids are excited by nothing non-electronic—lots of ways to go with that. To me their imaginative sense is deadened by video games, curiosity gene is just plain missin' in action."

"Tell you the truth, I haven't heard anyone *say* anything negative in the last few days. We finish up at Harpers Ferry and the Douglass homestead Monday. You sure you don't want to ride down to Petersburg for that reenactment?"

"That would be great fun Jalen but look, I have a ton of catching up to do on my painting. Ms. Carney's coming over tomorrow for her sitting. She can't sit still for a minute, and you know the kind of picky person she is; then I haven't even begun to do sketches and photos for Mrs. Chambliss. Besides, you'll be trampling all over the place trackin' down that Decatur Dorsey dude while I sit there bored to death. By the way, did Chambliss ever get the background information to you that you need for Tofu?"

"Chambliss. I keep asking myself questions about that dude. Shot me a curve on Tofu; still no background info, no student file, no data. Not because I haven't asked. Look, bring your sketch book baby, roll with the photos you already got of those chicks—we can grab some great seafood, some baked shad—c'mon."

"The great persuader. Tell you what, I'll teach you to sketch and then you can help me. You know what a drag it is to lug all that gear around."

"Yeah okay. Nope, have yet to see anything that describes her academic profile; kinda worried about what it might say," said Jalen giving her a hug and kiss. "Did you see my love note? Left it for you this morning."

"I love you baby. I can always tell when you want to sneak up on me," said Chelsea laughing. "You captivate me with charm—and a rose to boot. Your mom's taught you well."

"Check this out. I did hear some scuttlebutt from Kemo. Says Tofu's dad, that guy who owns Turk's Tavern, used to own all of that property around Ebenezer Cemetery—barn, cemetery and the Tavern. At one time, it was all one piece of property. Apparently, he lost the barn in divorce. That's probably when we saw the for sale sign. Nobody's getting up off the info on the court's decision about the girl, not even Grace. God only knows what the deal is with Dennison—I could wring her nappy neck."

"Well if anybody knows the nitty-gritty, it would be Grace."

"Yep. Mum's the word with Grace! Some of the kids say that there was knife-play involved last spring. A bunch of those Apôtre Chiennes blocked the door, while the leader tried to jack-up some girl—Damisi's friend."

"Best to wait on Chambliss."

"I think he made a mistake when he approved that *Apôtres* Chiennes Club; they sold themselves as a scholastic club for woman's excellence, but really are a gang. They asked for Dennison as their advisor and after that incident last spring, after the courts stepped in, he banished them from campus. Dennison continued to meet with them after that banishment, so he temporarily suspended her—several of us confirmed that we'd seen her around town, off campus, with group members.

"She still met with them—that's on her."

"I know, I was talking to somebody—can't remember who now, said that some of those graves at Ebenezer's go back to before the Civil War—said, 'might be some history right there waitin' for ya.' Heard some dudes singing out there the other day. Looked like they were diggin a grave—with all the shooting and killin' going on in D.C., that hole could be out there just waiting for anybody. Just think, the twenty-first century comes with anonymous graves out there waitin' for the next drive-by or sniper—or lunatic. Maybe we'll take Royce to the Tavern for dinner—give us a chance to check things out."

"So don't lose his card."

"Here, you take it—you're much more organized than me. I'll leave it under this candle."

The scent of lavender from the candle initiated a kiss that flickered long into the night, well past the striking cheekbones that voiced, 'shu-dooby, shuby doo' and blended in ambrosia with the felicitous, feline fingertips of Chelsea Harkness.

XIII

Spence was excited about the tour of Harpers Ferry. The trip to Thomas Circle had motivated him to research General Thomas, search for the Second Battle of Nashville and learn about how the African- American soldiers there initiated that battle against Hood. He felt proud of their spirited attack on Peach Orchard Hill, noting that the unlucky 13th USCT lost 40 percent of its unit; that pride fizzled at the thought of being stabbed and punctured by a bayonet. "Never read about that before," he thought exiting the school door.

"Man—don't think I could handle that," he thought as he took note of the tour bus waiting in front of the school. "Hey Mr. Kemo—you doing okay? Where's the regular school bus, the yellow one?"

"We're rolling in style today Spence," said Kemo, "Your teacher has a video that he wants to run while we go to Harpers Ferry—at least, that is what he told me yesterday. Yellow buses don't do video. Wants you guys to get warmed up on the relationship between Fred Douglass and John Brown. Going to take us little over an hour to get there, so I figure he's got a captive audience."

"Oh man, can I see inside?"

"For a minute. Soon as you take a short gander, run inside and tell everybody I'm out here waitin'."

When Spence came out of the tour bus, his eyes were as big as the tires on the bus. "Now that is a *movie* bus. I can hardly wait, Kemo; this is a tour for the books! "

"I sure hope so. You know, Teach is trying to help you guys prepare for adulthood, be ready to meet some challenges you might not understand along the way. I'm not sure all of your fellow students understand that; just try to absorb as much as possible of the things you see. One day you might appreciate some of what you don't understand at first glance."

"Got it!"

The bus had pulled out after loading the class. Jalen took the rollcall and welcomed the students once they reached I-495.

"Good morning ladies and gentlemen. I hope you enjoyed yesterday's tour to see General Thomas and Mr. Lincoln. I want you to know that I appreciate the enthusiasm and deportment that you displayed yesterday. Today we are off to see Harpers Ferry and the Douglass Mansion in southeast D.C. Our time with Mr. Douglass may be short as it takes a while to get to Harpers Ferry, but we will do the best that we can. I brought along two short videos—one of John Brown and the other of Frederick Douglass. They will help you prepare for what you see today. Let's give a big hand to Mr. Kemo. He has graciously provided a tour bus for our ride today; let's show him our appreciation of his efforts."

"Yeah Kemo!! Many thanks Kemo! You the man Kemo!" peppered the bus aisle.

"Now be sure to take good notes during the ride, if you have questions send me a short note. No quizzes yet, I promise—but be ready, you never know when one might pop up!"

The movie started by explaining the importance of John Brown to the abolitionist movement. "John Brown was born in Connecticut. He was a friend of Frederick Douglass and recruited him to be party to a slave insurrection he planned in 1859. Many historians consider his actions leading up to this planned insurrection as the primary event leading to the American Civil War. The Fugitive Slave Act, a law passed in 1850, electrified the Abolitionist Movement; essentially, it mandated that escaped slaves be returned to slavery regardless of where they were found in the Union. One of Mr. Brown's heroes was minister and abolitionist Elijah Lovejoy, murdered by a pro-slavery mob, intent on destroying his printing press in Illinois.

"Question," blurted out the voice of Damisi at that point in the video, "What is an abolitionist?"

Kemo froze the video, tapped his corncob pie on the dashboard.

"Good question," said Jalen, from the front of the bus, "An abolitionist is a person who fought to have slavery abolished. Abolish means to get rid of, to banish—to prevent the existence of slavery."

The video resumed to discuss the failure of John Brown's raid on the arsenal, a place for storage of large caliber guns and ammunition, at Harpers Ferry. It continued with the capture of John Brown and his small forces, covered his inability to develop a slave insurrection and his ultimate capture and hanging by the future commander of Confederate forces, Robert E. Lee.

"That's why some of those slave songs mention John Brown's body. 'John Brown's Body Lies a-Moulderin'," sang a voice from the middle of the bus.

"My daddy says John Brown was one of the first white men to spill blood on behalf of black folk," said another. The merry debate drew to a close as the picturesque landscape of Harpers Ferry came into view. "Wow, look at the Potomac up here; it sure got kinda puny."

"You would be puny too if you had to travel all that way. Looks kinda rocky too, like some of those mountains fell in it. Hey, and look over yonder," yelled Spence, "those folks are over there wading in it and some of them are drownin'."

Jalen caught sight of a bevy of cameras and megaphones. He surmised that some film company was making a movie on a slim beach not far from the engine house used by Brown for his last stand. "Okay my friends, here we are. Be sure to stand with your tour buddy; Spence, you are our guide-on. We need you to lead our tour; use this USCT flag as our point of rally. Once our tour is finished, we'll gather right here by the old Baltimore and Ohio railroad tracks. You can get some beautiful pictures from that point."

The history class from Claremont High dismounted the tour bus in a silent stupor. Arrested by physical majesty, necks craned, they slow-scanned the scene of Brown's horrific hanging; the disjunct metaphor overpowered adolescent comprehension. From the moment their feet gripped the ground, each imagination froze, transfixed.

"Man, look at that mountain over there; how would you like to slide down the side of that thing?"

"Not me; next time I come out here, I want to ride the train," exhorted from their mouths after they had taken the site tour. Jalen was more captivated by their reactions to the geography of the scenery, than to ancient ordnance facility itself. "How many of these kids have even been outside of D.C.?" he wondered.

"Excuse me sir, I noticed that you are in charge of several students, of this class visiting the grounds." The voice that momentarily startled him continued, "I have some students here myself—from Howard University. You might have noticed some of the cameras, actors and crew we have assembled out on that pebble beach. We're doing a filming of a slave episode. Please forgive me, Kashon Harley. I teach on the faculty at Howard University in the District. We're doing a filming of an incident that occurred at Ebenezer Creek, close to Savannah, Georgia. I was wondering if we could borrow some of your students—they might have to do some speaking?"

"You mean on camera? Some of them might enjoy that. "Jalen," he extended his hand, "Jalen Harkness."

"Would you select a few you think might be interested?"

"Tell you what, I'll call them over and you can pitch the opportunity; that way, you can get an idea of their maturity also. Some of them are kinda green." They both laughed, "Pleased to meet you."

"Okay folks," shouted Jalen, "Some of you may have noticed those cameras over there. Those are college students wading in the water, others carrying bundles on their heads and such. They are students from Howard University reenacting a scene—a historical scene that this gentleman will tell you about. It is about an incident that happened close to Savanna, Georgia. Professor Harley will explain it all to you; he wants to use some of you in the scene—thinks that a few of you might be *born* actors—a scene that portrays a betrayal. Listen up and he will explain."

"Good morning young people. This incident—some call it the "Betrayal at Ebenezer Creek"—involves Jefferson C. Davis, a Union general who used pontoons for his troops to cross Ebenezer Creek and then took the pontoons up before black war refugees—then called contraband—could *cross* the creek. The creek was ten feet deep, icy, and 165 feet wide; this was on Dec. 3, 1864. Some historians think that as many as a thousand slaves may have drowned, been killed, or captured in this incident. The slaves followed Union troops for protection and sought northward passage. Davis was part of Sherman's army—the army that rampaged through Georgia and then up through North Carolina. These slaves had cleared bushes, chopped trees, cooked, ironed, and washed to enable that army to attack the countryside, burning, pillaging and waging war on crops, Confederate forces, and rebel sympathizers in those states. As the Union troops made their way through Georgia, the Africans and African-Americans followed and assisted the Federals in any way they could, serving as teamsters, scouts, cooks and washerwomen. We are filming a part of that episode and we need one speaker and some African-American faces in the background—just more people. You might have to take off those ties and coats; ditch your shoes. Can you guys help us?"

"This is your movie opportunity for those of you who think you're good-lookin'," said Jalen.

"We have one speaking part for a young lady. I need to have three or four of you read it out loud and we will choose a person from that reading. Any volunteers for that? I'll read it and then you can decide if you want to tackle the part," said Harley.

"Go on up there Damisi," whispered Spence, "You're the best reader in the class. That part is probably made for you."

Harley started, "See there daddy—done told you that them Union soldiers couldn't be trusted. And after all that elbow grease y'all done wasted on their sorry behinds. Now they done pulled up dat bridge; made it disappear just as if it were magic. Johnnie Seccesh not real far behind; too skeered to tackle the blues, but not too afeared to rain hell on us as soon as they be able. Now what are we gonna do?"

"I can read that," thought Tofu, "Might just raise my stock with the Apôtre Chiennes—show up that Damisi;" *there goes her hand up in the air.*

"Here's the daddy, right here—the gentleman with the white hair,"continued Harley. "Whose my first contestant?"

From beside several bystanders, curious about the filming and unfamiliar with the drama historically, Constance viewed the proceedings. She nudged Mary Land saying, "Betcha we gits some fireworks right here on this water."

Damisi stepped to Professor Harley, studied the text momentarily, and launched into her reading. "See there daddy...I done *told* you that them Union soldiers couldn't be trusted! And after all that elbow grease y'all done wasted on their sorry behinds. Now they done pulled *up* that bridge;" and she jerked her hand upwards towards the West Virginia mountains, "made it disappear just as if it were," and whispered, '*magic*.' Johnnie Succesh not real far behind, too skeered to tackle the blues, but not too afeared to rain hell on us, soon as they are able," she raised her eyes skyward, "Now what are we gonna do?"

"Very good. Anyone else?" The bystanders clapped as the young students nodded their approval, proud of the energetic display.

Tofu waddled up to the smiling professor. She waved the text heroically and started. "S..s..See there daddy...I done told you dat them Union soldiers couldn't...uh..uh..uh...be trusted." Several students shifted their weight uneasily; looks of embarrassment crept through both class and crowd. "And after *all* that uh...uh...elbow grease y'all done wasted on their sorry behinds. Now they done yanked up that b-br-bridge; made it d-d...disappear, just as if it were majesty. Johnnie Seccesh not real far behind; too skeered to tackle the blues, but not too—a...ah...afeared of us to rain hell on us as *soon* as they be able." Shaking her head, she cried, "Now what am we gon' do?" A bleak and noticeable quiet greeted her performance; Harley hurriedly took both girls aside, awarding Damisi the role and Tofu a visible non-speaking role. Conrad, eyes closed, hands cupped, and mouth covered strained to repress a gut-giggle.

XIV

Dammit, that girl stuck her hand up, gritted her teeth, and made the effort to read the script. Gotta show her that I appreciate the effort. The question is how? It cannot sound flimsy or cheap; she's too uptight for that. Can't be superficial either; that might lose her. She's on the damn fence. Just a straightforward question. Jalen was afraid that a malformed question would turn any conversation with Tofu down a bizarre path, result in a defense laden with macabre allegories, fallacious recriminations, facetious tales, lies. *Best not tread down that path. What does the landscape look like on either side—go gang-land on one side, drop out on the other maybe. She's on the fence I really need to examine her academic dossier. Take it home...get some feedback from Chelsea. At least she wants to compete. Damisi brings that out in her. Not now though; wait for the seminal moment—one most opportune and casual.*

"Okay folks, be sure you got all your stuff. Good show back there and you got a great double-douse of information..John Brown and Ebenezer Creek. I love it; hope you do too. Principal Chambliss lined us up with some box lunches—ham sandwiches, turkey, chicken and chips—sodas too, topped off with?"

"Milk? Donuts? O.J.," came back in a vocal, asymmetrical array.

"No, an apple!," said Jalen. *There she goes again into her cocoon, hood over the head, earphones plugged in—sulk her way to the next stop. Need an opening, both opportune and accidental; don't say a damn thing now.*

"An apple," was met with groans.

"Remember, apples are good for your teeth," said Jalen adding, "Did you enjoy our Harper's Ferry trip?"

"Yes!" roared from the passenger compartment; Jalen smiled.

"Now," obviously pleased with the response and in mode majestic, he continued, "for our last stop on the tour, we are headed to southeast D.C. Okay, listen up folks—I know that a lot has happened and Harpers Ferry deserves a ton of discussion, but this is important. So, let me have your full attention up here. The Douglass Mansion is not in the very best of neighborhoods. *Can't say shit to her, although the others have noticed that she is in a world all by herself.* Spence, tap Tofu—let her know that we need her attention. Anyway, the Mansion is not in the best of 'hoods. We will take the tour—the folks there are expecting us. Then we'll head back to school. Any questions?"

"Okay, as you were—oh, one last thing. Spence, hold up that USCT 13th flag. Once more, this is our rally point. Try not to get separated from the group. Stay together and remember to check on your buddy. Are we missing anyone? Do I need to call the roll? I'll call it anyway." *Somehow, I get the feeling that this girl has been terrorized—history of the black race—stolen or terrorized. Black folk used to terror—ain't nothing new to them. Their kids accept it as a matter of course, part of the price of livin'.*

"Teach—you sound like a tour guide," said Anthony.

90

"Thank you Tony; I'm your permanent, in-school tour guide. Now, Douglass had personally experienced the brutality and lack of personal sovereignty that accompanied slavery; he was *born* a slave and campaigned against it. Long before there were books teaching reading and computerized reading tutors, Mr. Douglass taught himself to read. Remember—can you all hear me? We can turn the microphone up if not—Ebenezer Creek. That incident occurred at almost the same time, to the day, that the USCT 13th was fighting Hood's Confederates in Nashville; it was icy at Ebenezer Creek and it was icy and freezing in Nashville. If fact, General Thomas was almost fired for delaying his attack on Hood. Some of you know that I am headed to Petersburg to do my own research on African-American Decatur Dorsey, medal of honor winner in the Battle of the Crater. I cannot find one word that Decatur Dorsey uttered in print. I have found an interview with Moses Slaughter, black veteran of The Battle of Nashville. We need to thank Mr. Douglass each and every day for his witness and writing—newspapers, three autobiographies, speeches. The Douglass Mansion is in the Cedar Hill section of Anacostia. *Hadn't meant to talk this long; Jeez, hope I don't turn them off with all this chatter. I must be inspired or sumpthin'.*

"You guys have seen a bunch of statues by now, not a whole lot of them honor women; even fewer honor African-Americans. Fact of the matter is, you can almost gauge the diversity, the intellectual climate of a town in these United States by the number of statues it has honoring its black citizens—those who have fought as soldiers, writers, and as garbage workers, for fairness and diversity. I'll shut up after I say one more thing—aim for being citizens of the world. Don't use our white brethren as your model; you can do better than that! When you deliver your reports, think about how artists—sculptors, musicians, poets—commemorate those presidents and generals whose memorials we have visited."

"I like *your* reports better," said Damisi, "it goes well with these apples."

91

"Thank you 'Misi, I just got a little inspired."

"Your next life, you are gonna be a preacher Jalen," said Kemo.

"Well if I wasn't a jacked-up learner myself, I wouldn't be in this business, wouldn't be trying to ignite some curiosity! Say that word out loud for me folks...curiosity!"

"Curiosity!" roared back at him from smiling, yelling lips. "I'll sit down now—thanks for listening."

"You get any more hopped-up about Brown and Douglass, you 'll make this bus look like it's a part of "Soul Train" brother Harkness. Well you know they put all those early fighters against slavery in the crazy category; Nat Turner, John Brown—schizophrenic fools, religious zealots, mad-hatters one and all."

"I guess I'm just excited, trying to get these kids to be my partners in the excursion to the past, and their heritage—our heritage—the greatness of their forefathers, mothers too."

The video that filled the balance of the trip discussed the many times Douglass met with Lincoln to urge arming of the slaves as soldiers for the Union. In another thirty minutes, the bus pulled up to the Douglass Mansion. The students had rolled down their pant legs, refitted their shoes, and "dressed back up" during the bus ride.

"Good luck with your esteem builder, Douglass-style," said Kemo.

"Hey man, once the scaffold is built, I'm betting that these folks take off. Gotta let Tofu know that I appreciate her effort back there at the ferry. I got a bit of a different take on her issues there. 'kay young people, line up behind Spence; the tour guides spotted us, know we have arrived.

Remember those pictures and sketches, take good notes and use your phone's tape recorder if you have a smart-phone.

"Good morning boys and girls; we are very happy to have you students here to day. I am the guide for your tour of the Douglass Mansion. Frederick Douglass was born Frederick Bailey in 1818. By virtue of personal effort, he became a leading abolitionist, writer, and diplomat. Douglass wrote three autobiographies, held several government posts, and was married four times.

"Look Damisi, there is one pair of his glasses right there," said Roland. "Can we take pictures of the library?" asked Roland of the tour guide.

"Yes, but only *without* flash. Now, Douglass lost sons in the American Civil War and one of his grandsons became a prominent violinist on the international scene. He was a great lover of music and owned a piano in addition to a voluminous library. I understand that you guys were up at Harpers Ferry this morning. John Brown and Mr. Douglass maintained a strong friendship; it was not unusual to hear the "Battle Hymn of the Republic," sung to the tune of "John Brown's Body" right here in this living room."

"Douglass let his grandson be a violinist—thought violin was for sissies," said Roland under his breath.

"Whisperin' is for sissies Roland. Sh—shsh!," countered Constance.

"These are some of the original pots and pans used for cooking in the Douglass household, and out back many of you will want to look at the Growlery, reconstructed in the nineteen eighties. Douglass had a wonderful sense of humor and loved to tease and growl like a lion' when he was writing. He'd be out there pacing and talking to himself. Nowadays we call that role-playing."

"How many of you have read anything by Douglass? Okay, that's a fair number. I love this one passage by Mr. Douglass—'with all your religious parade and solemnity, you are to him, mere bombast, fraud, deception, impiety, and hypocrisy.' Write those words down and see how the sentence finishes. You can find those words on the Internet. Any questions? If not, explore the grounds a bit, and thank you for coming."

"Ten minutes folks, then we line up behind Spence."

"I have a question—Douglass lost sons in the Civil War and argued for slaves to fight for their freedom as Union soldiers, right? And then he let one of his grandsons play the *violin*?" queried Anthony.

"Well in some neighborhoods, playing the violin is an activity frowned upon by the stupid and bully wannabes. Where I come from, it takes a warrior be superlative at anything, from playing the violin to playing football. In fact, let me play something for you," said the tour guide taking the violin to his chin and rendering Bellstedt's "Variations on Dixie."

"My goodness, that was a virtuoso performance," said Jalen, adding "let's have a big, big hand for our tour guide." The class gave the guide a thunderous ovation. "Back to the bus in five minutes."

Jalen quick-scanned the audience, nodding to Kemo to ready the bus. Many of the class members went out to view the "Growlery" and soon growls, groans, and grunts came from that backyard location.

"I'm a black lion with a huge afro," teased Anthony,. "I look like you guys in the sixties. 'Grrrr' Teach."

"I'm Frederick's bush on steroids," answered Constance. In the background, a distant siren whined as the students, captured in their

94

own Douglass rhapsody, bantered and chanted, imitating Douglass in role-play. "Gonna growl like this when I write my report; read it out loud!"

"Let's go people," ordered Jalen, "the bus is out front and it's getting close to shutdown time at school and traffic..."

A loud screech of car tires sounded, as if a turn had been taken too fast. Sirens kept sounding as if getting closer. "Grrrr...I 'm a lion scion!"

"It's picking us up—Spence, hold that flag high, stand right next to the front porch, so they can form..."

"Bang, bang!!"

"Rat-tat-tat...Rat-tat-tat!!!"

"That sounds close. What's going on, where's that coming from...?"

Gunshots reported, as confusion swept the body of students. Bang, bang, bang!!! Rat-tat-tat!!!

"Down, down everybody! Hug the ground...down. Spence, down down. *Jeez*. Oh my god—dooooooown, DOOOOOOWN!!!!"

A cardinal red Pontiac, its left rear tire in reckless wobble and rolling on rims smoking from implosion, made "W" Street a perilous theater—stage left, stage middle, stage right—in seconds. It grazed the bus, ricocheted, bounced-off and ping-ponged curbs, side-swiped several parked cars, and screamed around the corner one half block away with police cars whining in hot pursuit. Notebooks, notepads, loose paper, dropped cameras and smart-phones littered the front lawn of the Douglass Mansion. Tour guides, bent and wobbly, scurried like frantic, berserk geese furiously checking young students for bloodied body eruptions. Harkness' Claremont students lay sprawled across an autumnal lawn like fallen leaves, some silent, some crying, some shaking and wide-eyed in disbelief.

Jalen eye-balled the scene, scanning his students like a Mississippi minesweeper, ordering them to hug the ground in militant screams. *Damn!!!! The re-enactment isn't until next week; this sure as hell looks like a war zone. Shit..Oh..oh,* "Shit!!!" *The bus—check the bus.* "Kemo— Kemo...oh no, Kemooooo!!!!!!!"

XV

"I'm off babe…save my place right here beside you for tonight; gotta get over to school early—forgot to set the clock."

Her eyes still closed, Chelsea mumbled, "Love you honey, hmmmm—have a great day and be careful." She rolled on her side. "I'm so glad you're okay, after all that stuff down in southeast, down at the Douglass Mansion—you got in so late and looked so tired. I was relieved, glad when you got here. have you got to go in today; sure wish yo could stay here with me—uh, do you still want to go to dinner tomorrow?"

"Oh yeah…got it all setup. Don't getup, I'm already late; gonna stop and get coffee and donuts on the way." He kissed her forehead, nuzzled her neck, palmed her left shoulder; "Stay delicious."

Traffic was light as he held the speed limit slicing toward school; the girl at the window of the drive-thru said, "Four ninety-five, two cinnamon donuts and a hot coffee, one cream, one sugar."

"There you are Jalen!" The sound of Dennison's voice had a comic tremor in it, the energy of a panther poised to pounce. "My goodness, it seems like everything you do has drama in it; old Frederick got a Harkness tailwind yesterday, according to reports; you're a human hurricane careening across the front page of our hometown newspaper."

"Hey Dennison—newspaper? I haven't seen it yet. Fact is, I ran kinda late this morning and barely brushed my teeth. Anyway, I feel like I've been hit by one."

"Well that bit of excitement you had yesterday has the halls humming. Happy to see that you are okay. I brought in some extra copies; Grace is in the office inhaling the news

I brought in some extra copies; Grace is in the office inhaling the news as we speak—extra copies for Mr. Chambliss too. Goodness knows that you and the kids were so very lucky. Uh...I..."

"Thanks,"—*happy to see that I'm okay, bullshit!* "We were extremely fortunate; say, you gave Tofu some lessons over the summer, right? I think her mom mentioned that the last time she came in."

"Oh yes, poor girl. I installed some software on her mom's, on Queen Esther's computer, and had her work it for comprehension and vocabulary. I had her do some speed work too. Is there a problem?"

He posed his question to navigate the space in the change of pitch. "No, no problem. I am trying to get a fix on her level of performance. I did get that file from Chambliss, but am curious—what do you think of her progress? I mean, how well do you think she performs with respect to her grade level?"

"Well it's all in her file: all of her comprehensive tests, how to interpret her scores! You do understand how to interpret those scores, do you not? The correlations are pretty straightforward; however, you *do* have to read the fine print."

"Yes, but what do you think? Is the problem more with her vision, stuttering or some sort of elocution issue as opposed to concentration or comprehension?"

"Well I'd be interested in what you come up with. For my part, I think the child is just a bit slow, if you know what I mean. Surely, you haven't discussed this with the mother?" replied Dennison.

"Oh no! Did you have her do any fluency stuff? Something beyond the software, perhaps reading...?"

"Oh Jalen, I really must be on my way—and remember to stay out of the way of those bullets."

"Out loud," he said to her back, almost silently bidding her good-bye. Jalen fish-eyed the hallway and made his way to the main office,

"Hi Grace, is Primus around?"

"Morning Mr. Harkness. Oh yes, he is around, in fact, he just went down the hall looking for you.

Gone!! Jalen's heart skipped into a moonwalk, almost freeing his curiosity to banter; *Grace, Grace—two time winner of the D.C. beauty-race, office parliamentarian in satin and lace.* He said, "Whassup with Dennison? What is it? I bumped into her just now; cannot get a fix on her perception of Tofu. I'll go find Chambliss. Do you know what he wants? "

"Jalen, after all that rigmarole yesterday. Even you can figure out what he wants; read my lips, think paperwork!!! Take a look at this front page news; 'Anacostia Anarchy Decks Students.'"

The foreground of the picture beneath the headline showed a back shot of Jalen, his necktie waving furiously in the breeze, his feet a foot off the ground, while wrestling two students ground-ward. Between the middle ground and background of the photograph, students lay sprawled in terror stricken disarray. In the far distance of the photo, the flag of the USCT13[th] reigned unfurled, arcing over an onslaught of paper, plastic bags, fallen leaves, and unsavory detritus, knocked over from automobile-spanked trash cans. The longer he looked, the more gunshots seemed to roar.

"Y'all were almost Anacostia Toast," said Grace.

"Yeppy—it was not pretty, not funny either. Can I have one of those? Look though, before I forget—I think I have Kemo's cell number; just in case, would you give it to me."

"No problem. Be sure to add it to your contacts. Jalen, you know the drill. This is the incident report paperwork Chambliss needs from you, and he needs it *today.* Be a dear and get it back to me asap. Just between you and me, Dennison foams at the mouth when she *hears* your footsteps; she doesn't have to hear your name, see you; be careful around her. I'm certain she thinks you were behind that suspension she got last spring. She can be real mean, kick up a ton of dust. Backstabber!"

"Hey, if her hiss had poison in it, I'd be a dead man. She doesn't or won't let on about her techniques and approaches she used with Tofu. Has she given you any comments regarding her summer sessions with that girl?"

"Get serious, she's in a world of her own. I stay away from her; she uses Tofu's academic record like a sword ready to slice Chambliss up if she can. Just don't talk with her, leave her alone. Look, you guys had a close call yesterday; things could have been much, much worse. She left this with me—she wants the entire file back as soon as you are finished with it. The Park Service called to commend your leadership and collegiality yesterday—that's a good thing. And Jalen, thanks in advance for getting on top of that paperwork; I appreciate it."

On the way to his classroom, Jalen dialed the number Grace had given him.

"Hey man, whassup! Thought I would call and check on you, seeing as how you be the hero and all," said Jalen.

"Me? You got the hero role lil' brother. I'm looking at that shot one of the kids got of you diving across some of those students; you could a been a linebacker or somethin', moving around like that."

"Me—ha-ha. But I didn't take the blow bro. Look, Chelsea and I are headed to Turk's place tomorrow night—dinner, drinks, whatever. Been thinking that I should talk to him about his daughter. Whadoyou think?"

"He's a full course Jalen; a power package. Kinda like carrying dynamite in a buckboard, you dig. Big, burly white guy, Confederate flag over the fireplace—I mean, I would think twice. Speaking of blows,
 this blow ain't forever, thankfully just a flesh wound, a crease in the shoulder—could have been worse."

"Say what?"

Connection bad...move past the lockers, "I said I didn't take the blow—just a flesh wound. Doc says they want to observe me for a day or two, then I'm outta here."

"Your bus didn't look so good, last I saw it. The rangers kept the Douglass place open until we got out of there. We were there until almost seven o'clock, filing out reports and all. Took statements from all the students. Your folks got us a bus out there around 6:45 pm. I'm headed to class; we probably won't get much done today, given the excitement from yesterday and all. Keep me informed!"

"Will do, thanks for checking."

The students were surprisingly relaxed and convivial when he arrived.

"Good morning Mr. Harkness. We know you are glad to see our smiling faces. Thank you for your –orders!" The unison chant had hit him full face as he crossed into the classroom; his chest broadened, some would say exploded, and his face stretched into a big smile. "Ha-ha-has," streaked across the classroom.

"You people are awesome. Mr. Chambliss must have put you guys up to this. Actually, I should thank you. You performed admirably under very stressful conditions. All of that intelligence—musta come from the Douglass library—the books, the piano, the violin. All Douglass' curiosity and luminescence did not go wasted on you guys."

"Grrrrrr!" teased Anthony, crouched behind his seat exulting Douglass mania.

"Mr. Harkness...what does luminescence mean?"

"It means a light in the darkness...like the moon at night, like the glow of the moon or lighthouse on the shore. I have a favorite painting—it's in the Edinburgh National Art Gallery. It's called "Allegory" and was painted by El Greco. It's a powerful rendition of the magnetism of a story, a tale. To me, Douglass is that light, that beacon of personality that enchants and illumines—lights up darkness. And he does it without heat. So you guys followed instructions yesterday and undoubtedly, you and your parents saw these photos. Looks like a war zone; we were there just to learn about our history, the heroes in our culture, and how they informed and gathered themselves to face challenges—old and new. "Spence...come up here! Folks, yesterday I thought I had already gone to Petersburg for a minute, then I remembered, that is NEXT week. I want you to look at that flag waving there in the background. That is how we knew where to fall down, how to stay unified and together. Spence got that flag waving up in the air; the luminary—the light in this photo is the flag. Look at all that garbage floating around—paper, plastic bags, cereal boxes, newspapers—that flag guided us in the storm. Spence, you get the Decatur Dorsey Award for the week. Now, let's get started on your reports today. I'll give you free time starting now to outline your ideas. You can mind-map them if you want. Any questions?"

"Oh, Tofu...would you step here a minute? Look, I…"

"My mother made me do it, Mr. Harkness—I didn't want to!"

"Made you do what Tofu?"

"Send in the pictures—the one that ended up in the newspaper!"

"You took those? I knew it had to be one of you guys; but that's okay. They were excellent pictures. The police may need pictures of the actual events as they happened. What you did is a good thing. And also, you made a great effort yesterday at Harpers Ferry; so you had quite a day on BOTH counts. Not to worry. On another note, do you have any scores from the software you worked on this past summer? If so, I sure would like to see them."

At day's end, he took the completed forms to the office, gathered Tofu's dossier, and called Chelsea. "Babe, I'll get some carryout dinner for tonight—Chinese or something—just...I need you to be there with your ears; I need your feedback on a few things. I'll bring a bottle of our favorite wine too."

"Glad to be the one, dear—you just point your old trusty self this way. Me and my ears, we'll be here waitin'."

XVI

"You're treating me like a queen—dinner out tomorrow night, brought dinner home tonight; Queen Esther ain't got nothing on me."

"You *are* a queen—my queen. Bring me those lips, those hips, gimme some brainy, zany quips!" They nuzzled into a long, warm kiss. "Baby, you look great in that robe; and to think that I married all this! I love it when you send me these sexy messages."

"Naw, you love sexy massages."

"Okay egg foo-young for you; got some hot tea too." They hugged on the sofa, forked foo-young, exchanged slurpy, sloppy kisses. Jalen rubbed her knees while chomping. "Chelsea look, here is Tofu's cumulative record—test scores, evaluations, scores on various reading and math tests. Dennison didn't give me much info on her approach with Tofu over the summer. I did ask Tofu to bring in any scores she might have on that reading software she worked on. Looks like reading might be a problem—another parent turn-over—learning left to the school's teaching staff; like parents have no role to play."

Chelsea crept up under his chin, her arms around his waist. "Still hot—thanks for the reprieve honey. This is good, real good. Let's put the file on the coffee table—keep it grease free. Do you think she might be dyslexic? Has she been tested for that?" She speared another forkful of rice.

"Not as far as I know. Nothing in her file indicates dyslexia. Grace told me to be careful with Dennison; said she—how did she put it—could, "kick up a ton of dust." How does that resonate with you—kick up dust? Hey, this hits the spot. Got it at Rice King's."

"Well, I think she's right. Dennison reminds me of a dog with a bone; just won't turn loose. I had a student like your Tofu once, when I did my student teaching; that can be a tough one to diagnose." She took a napkin, wiped the corner of his mouth. "I know what you mean about parents; they don't rely on teachers nowadays as guides, they are the whole show; parents expect teachers to control kids that they themselves cannot control. Weird."

Jalen knocked back a swig of wine. "I haven't got the impression that Dennison knows a whole lot about reading; the system doesn't really have reading teachers like the old days. She may have had Tofu reading out loud, maybe. Some of that software measures comprehension. You know, if you question reading as a skill, some folks get real defensive," he spoke in high-pitched, street mode. "You stupid or somethin'—shit, I can read"—like *fuck-you* from jump street. Never get to say, quality or quantity. Many parents never heard of using software to help reading, identify issues, test comprehension. Let me taste those lips again baby. Chelsea-a-la foo-young—wow." He fisted his elbow downward.

"Well, my parents were adamant about reading. They quizzed us on what we read. Software wasn't around then. Memphis had a one room schoolhouse for blacks until 1950; school right there on President's Island—on stilts, no less. The town oozes illiteracy."

"You lucked out. Tofu says she has a computer. There was this group from Howard at Harper's Ferry yesterday making a film. They wanted some additional folks to play roles in a documentary of an incident that took place in North Carolina—Ebenezer Creek. They wanted extras, so Damisi read some of the script. Tofu too."

"I know Damisi jumped all over that. How'd Tofu do?"

"Stumbled and tripped all over the place; sounded like a third or fourth grader. But look," he showed Chelsea the dossier, "her comprehension scores are at the 8th grade level. I think something else is working."

"If there is, I know you will help her deal with it. Hey, I forgot to tell you—mom and dad called, said your picture is plastered all over the front page of today's paper. I meant to go out and get one, but ended up sketching landscapes. It was kinda dusty outside—breezy with long shadows—and dust from the leaves sparkled in afternoon sunlight. Great weather for sketching. Said one picture makes you look like you were about to go into superman mode." She raised the glass to her lips, taking a long sip.

"Hey, I wasn't the one; Spence—that kid carried the flag, held that flag right up; cool and calm just like a veteran. The other kids didn't panic either. I am so proud of them; they sang me a tune as I walked in class today. I might just put a computer and some reading software in my classroom; use it to check reading all on my own. I got some bruises here and there: elbow, knee, shoulder. Speaking of bruises, I could stand a good massage. More rice? Wine?"

"No, all good here; foo-young goes well with this Pinot Grigio you brought. Here's a napkin, you've got some rice on the side of your mouth. Here, let me kiss it off you."

"Now that feels sooo good."

"You are sooo welcome. There's more in store where that came from."

"From the heart?"

"A shower of heart dust, for starters."

"Do you think we make a good love team?"

"Well you gave me a nice back rub the other day. Why don't we put on some nice music, close up things in the kitchen, make sure all the doors are locked, and we can investigate our team play. Let me work on seeing what's under this robe."

"Ooohh, gooody. Marvin Gaye would be perfect right about now, maybe a little 'What's Going On'; dance?" She held out her hand, hoisted him up from the sofa, kneaded her fingers into the brown muscles around his neck. "We danced like this on one of our first dates. You remember?"

"If I didn't you would never let me hear the end of it. Of course I remember. Now, do you remember what I said in response?"

"Without a doubt. You said, 'there is no one around who can't guess that we are lovers; those sharp of sense see all that love dust, smell those love embers burning, and hug jealousy.'"

"Nope. I said, your fingers and arms are real warm and making me hot and zealous. Now, since you got me all hot and zealous, how 'bout that 'Rescue Me' you promised." After checking the doors, restarting Mr. Gaye, losing his clothes, and starting the shower, Jalen jumped in, Chelsea followed. "Watch out for the knee—it's still a little sore." Chelsea lathered his back, soaped his neck and teased taut nipples against his spine. "That feels good, real good. I think I got a little buzz going."

"Me too—we should do this more often. I love you Jalen; I don't say that enough, but I love being with you, around you. I think I love you more now than when we married."

"What do I need to do, to make sure you stay that way; that's a good thing. Whew, your fingers are strong."

"I thought of you—on an off today; we make love differently now than when we first got married."

"You think so? In what way?"

"I almost think you have a thermometer or something in your—*johnson.* It's just that you seem to understand more about how my wires work. Strange in a way, because I never really thought of myself as having the kind of sexual energy that you bring out in me." A flash of energy charged her heart, a muscle in her lip quivered. Eyes closed, Chelsea steadied her knees, turned Jalen around by the shoulders. "Rescue Me," floated from her throat, danced in the warm mist. "It's like my body sometimes just screams for you to be within." Warmed by the shower' s heat, she kissed his chest, fisted *mr. johnson.* "It's not that we weren't good at first; it was more physical in a way. Now, oh shucks—you know what I mean—it's in your silences, in the way you touch me—I trust you more."

Jalen pulled her close and held her quietly inhaling the sound of the shower water. Finally he said, "That's because I do love you Chelsea, I love you. Talking about it doesn't make it stronger, or better; and I appreciate your journaling with me—that is important to me. I love this mood, this halo or whatever it is; I never want it to go away." Agility, grace, and tenderness claimed the mood, as Jalen Harkness fingered the spot most moist in her under-body; he felt her tremble, brace, shudder slightly.

"Okay, how's your shoulder?"

"I'm going to dry off now."

Chelsea lingered in the shower long enough to dry her tears. *I don't know what's happening with me, saying all this stuff, pouring out my heart. Seems like I'm on pins and needles ever since I left teaching and decided to major in creativity, paint full time. I haven't spoken to anyone like this since I was in high school, maybe since I started having my period.* She assumed an air of confidence as she strolled to the bedroom. Jalen lay parked comfortably on two pillows; he held her in his arms for several minutes.

"You must think I'm nuts, carrying on like this about love and loving. I mean—after all, we've been married for almost three years now. Surely I'm used to being around you by now—and you have been very supportive, especially since we talked, about starting the art studio. Do you think I am too sensitive?"

Nerve scouts shot through every fiber and inch of his body; they spoke to him in nanoseconds. Almost anything can be interpreted negatively or positively; he thought of business development as a puzzle, not a problem, dialed through degrees of discretion, tact—angles of political correctness. Positive brain scout cautioned; *turn it back man, let her answer it; you think long, you think wrong, bro.* Negative brain scout chimed in; *tell her you love her, nothing else unless you want second guessing and crying all night.* A brain scout from the synthesis school offered; *look puzzled, stutter, and speak slowly.*

"That's is a great question Chelsea, great—and I think that you are the only person in this room that can answer it." The word "it" was his cue to grab her and give her a big kiss on the forehead; he added a compliment on her beauty and sincerity, saying. "Chelsea, I don't know what I would do without you."

"You're sure about that shoulder?"

"Better, much better. I've never been called a thermostat—a thermometer before. Mr. Johnson has been called a lot of things before, but never a thermostat.

"Come over here mister 'T.' Come over and meet miss 'C.'"

There was much combustion, tons of emotion, and sparkling tenderness in both miss "C" and doctor "T" that night. Doctor "T" plumbed the depths of miss "C," careful to take accurate temperature, lest he foam and fizzle. Miss "C" rose to heights of ecstatic pleasure and reckless enthusiasm, while taking great pains to rein in the fingernails of her owner. T.C. in D.C! In the quietude of their aftermath, both participants thought, *oooohhh baby, you are so delicious!*

XVII

"Hey Chelsea...made some coffee! It's still hot—you interested?"

"Yes—sounds good, look I have an idea."

"Okay," Jalen rounded the door jam, and on the night table rested the cup, "coffee, cream and sugar for your pleasure."

"Look, I have an idea for Tofu—I want to deliver it myself, plus I can add a little spice to what you are already doing with your class. So I dreamed last night that I presented a talk on art—how artists, sculptors and the like, represent heroes in their work using gestures and small artifacts—hats, eyeglasses, cigars, books...that sort of thing. It's interesting stuff—I could stop by for a minute or two today. It might help them with their presentations. What do you think?"

"Come by today? Great honey, bring it on. They would enjoy that. The tour class meets at one—can you make it then?"

"No problem, I'll come by then." When Chelsea walked into the class, the students were very surprised and elated. They were in small groups, discussing their individual skills, writing, drawing, speaking, and defining procedures during their group reports.

"Good morning young people. It's wonderful to be here with you today," said Chelsea, "Mr. Harkness invited me to spend some time with you; he thought that you might need a change of pace." Beside her stood an easel, a white canvas covering a large, rectangular object, and a silver platter covered with marshmallows. "I understand that you have been on a tour of various Civil War sites in and around the Washington, D.C. area. As some of you know, I am the wife of Mr. Harkness."

A flurry of chatter met that statement and a few eyes scrutinized Jalen's smile.

"At one time, I taught in the Prince George's County school system. Right now, I am taking some time away from teaching so that I can develop and produce my own work—some paintings, some sketches and sculpture that I can sell. My idea is to create art that looks both forward and backwards—works that reflect the African-American experience and raises some questions about its future. From my discussions with your teacher, I understand that you are enjoying your visits to various sites. Often, we refuse to examine slavery; for our ancestors, parents, grand and great-grandparents, it was a terrible and painful period that they didn't want to think about. But it is the heritage of our country and we are a testament to the strength of human heart and mind. I think we have arrived at a time when we can use that history as a resource—its music, its art and food, its stories, and yes, its battles—yes, its battles of head, heart, mind, and body. Can you all hear me?"

"Yes ma'am," echoed in varied beats in the classroom, which beamed with shining light and mostly smiling faces. Between the first and last echo, Chelsea placed four marshmallows, two on each side,
in the corners of her mouth. If our fore-bearers could only see us now; standing at this threshold, strong and vigorous, ready to partake of the human dream, ready to learn and develop our talents and skills in ways that were *verboten*, forbidden to them. The artist speaks in sights, sounds and movement to share unique visions of the world. Take that

word 'verboten'—a German word—which comes to life in pictures of segregated lunch counters.

"Can you hear me now?" she said, with marshmallows stuffed in her mouth.

Surprised at the contour of her mouth in its new state, the "Yes ma'am," of the students followed again.

"My dad was a principal in Memphis who believed in two broad principles—the scientific method and the worth and dignity of each individual. When I was growing up, he emphasized excellence and urged us toward that end in everything that we set out to accomplish. As black folk, we have consistently had barriers placed in our way to limit access to become full members, not just of the United States, but of the world community—be that in science, industrial arts, music, math, medicine—or in the humanities, the liberal arts. Can you understand me?"

"Uh-huhs," came in cacophony.

"Now you have seen sculptures, paintings, maps, libraries, and musical instruments on your tour. It took people—artists trained, developed, encouraged and refined to create these works, these works of beauty and message, to bring the soldiers and civilians that we honor, into being. They are pieces of art that memorialize those whose took great risks to develop the country we live in. When an artist has something to say, he or she will say it. Repeat that after me—when an artist..."

"When an artist has something to say, he or she will say it!" said the class.

"Excellent," said Chelsea..."Now I want you, in your reports that you do, to pay very close attention to the eyes, arms, hands, ears...the *posture* and gestures of everything—everything, you see as you recall your notes, sketches, and pictures you took. Are the ears perked? The tails of horses flowing? Does the man wear glasses as he reads? Is there a pen or ink on the table? Why does the general hold his hat in the wind or the President sit to listen, balance and seek justice? Why is a story or a drum important? All these things can be portrayed in art. So test ways that your sketches, poetry, songs—rap even, can make your reports come alive, to make them more memorable. Here is the painting that I made to share with you today."

Chelsea drew back the canvas covering her painting. An upturned galvanized garbage can stood in the middle of the oil painting, slightly right of center An upturned galvanized garbage can stood in the middle of the oil painting, slightly right of center. A bunch of long stemmed flowers—red roses, orange tulips, sunflowers, and purple wisteria—lay below the can, a third of the stems beneath the can's upper lip on an earthen landscape. "In one sentence, tell me what this means to you and give them to Ja—Mr. Harkness as you leave class."

"Okay," she said, taking the marshmallows out of her mouth. Some of our great dramatic artists, commonly called actors, use stones—I used marshmallows—in their mouths to improve their articulation. Can you say that word after me?"

"Ar-tic-u-la-tion," came in feisty rhythms.

"Okay, I want you to raise your hand if your church has a reading clinic."

One hand went up. "Mine does," said Spence.

"Raise your hand if you have a reading nook or library in your home." said Chelsea.

"Mine does," said Damisi raising her hand.

"Okay," said Chelsea continuing.

"Now, as you prepare for your presentations, remember this thought. The story of Africans in the Americas, especially in the democracy of the United States, is the singular story of human advancement in the nineteenth and twentieth centuries. It is a story of a fight against tribalism and as such is of tremendous importance. That story is *your* story; it is important. Don't let anyone steal it, pimp it, contravene, or demean it. In order to record it, you become *artistic* and sing, paint, write—you must read.

"Yes ma'am."

"Now, I am giving these marshmallows to Tofu; Tofu, take these unused marshmallows and practice speaking with them exactly like I did today—in the corners of your mouth. Use them with care."

***

Jalen gave his wife another big hug when he arrived home. "Wow Chelsea—you were inspired today. I stopped by the cleaners, to pickup my blue jacket for the reenactment—it made me skunk-whiffed when I wore it the last time. I spoke to Royce on the phone; he's all set for tonight. What should I wear, something casual or ya think kinda dressy?"

"You'll look dressy in a white shirt and tie, but maybe a casual jacket. I certainly don't think Turk's has a real formal dress code. I'm wearing this white blouse; here, you can have this hanger for your Union jacket. It's missing a button; give me a replacement and I'll sew it for you."

"Thanks hon'. You know, it's hotter than hell in that thing; can you imagine running around in July in it. Thankfully, they delayed things 'til the Fall—cotton and wool. I could lose twenty pounds in a day! I've read and reread transcripts of those congressional committees; they had a review of the Fort Pillow massacre—also had one to review events at the Crater. So, the one at Fort Pillow included the words of several blacks who survived the attack. Strange, because a Medal of Honor winner at the Crater, was *never* quoted. I still can't find one single, solitary word out of the mouth of Decatur Dorsey in print. Guess that wasn't unusual in the 1860s. Still, it would be interesting to get some idea of his mindset. Turk's is close to Ebenezer Hill. Kemo hipped me to his mindset—says he's hell on wheels, stocky and bald, slightly swarthy and looks like a old Irish bartender."

"Maybe he'll come around. He might be happy to talk to his daughter's teacher." He watched as Chelsea put on her earrings; he took as much pleasure in watching her dress as undress. There was method to it and effected as a sacred ritual. *Flourish.* "You look great babe."

"You always comment on this blouse; you must like what is in it—mister Harkness."

Jalen slid into a broadcloth white shirt, solid black tie, black blazer, tan slacks. "The weather folks think we might get some more rain, just enough to make it a bad hair night. I'll bring an umbrella. Speaking of Tofu, my hunch is she justs gets nervous; could be anxiety or maybe plain old stuttering. Chelsea sniffed two vials of perfume, chose Arpege, checked her hair in the mirror, and wriggled into a Duncan tartan skirt.

"How is Kemo anyway?"

"Says he'll escape the food in another day or so. Says the kids told him that Tofu looked like the original bullet train flying across the Japanese landscape. I think you're right about Tofu."

"That's not too unusual—lots of folks have that problem. Seems like Dennison would have picked up on it."

"Yeah." *She's a wily old bitch, chained to obscurity; verbal, logical, maybe emotional too—truly a refugee from the classroom.* "I have yet to get a straight answer from her." Once in the car, they headed past Catholic U, and east on Rhode Island. "Chelsea, you know the problem with trying to help these kids be able to compete, be successful learners is intergenerational."

"I know, white parents invoke more sophisticated barriers when black kids get close, especially around puberty—separate schools, then economically zoned community schools. Only heaven knows what comes after that. It begets colossal waves of communication ineptitude between races. Seems like they are intent on maintaining either an economic or educational edge. The violence in black communities doesn't help. Maybe the Internet might help these young black kids compete, especially for jobs in an international workplace."

"They want the best for their kids too; it is a challenging dilemma. But, fair is fair—children of color deserve the opportunity to compete; otherwise, the country has failed them. Then you get D.C. snipers or treason-oriented martyrs—extreme personality quirks."

What had been a drizzle-free ride became more wet and a harder rain as they approached the tavern.

"Okay—I'll let you out at the door. You take the umbrella."

"You'll have farther to walk...."

"Take it, I'm good."

Chelsea stood just inside the door; Jalen wiped his hands dry from the cold, wet raindrops he'd tried to dodge, duck, and zig-zag through. He dried his hands inside his pants pockets, fish-eyed the space, nodded to the maitre d",“Hey.”

“Greetings folks—getting a little wet out there. This way please,” said the maitre d’. They strode past a small bandstand, a bar which jutted out towards the entrance; refracted light from wine glasses sparkled and scrimmaged. Autographed photos of country music artists and un-autographed Confederate generals, dotted the walls.

“Thanks, this is fine. Looks like we….” the rumble of bass sounding thunder rolled through the room, causing the glassware to tinkle “just made it. Say, we’re expecting a…,” *maybe he's coming in drag,* “tall brown-skin guy to join us—Harkness is the name here.”

“You think he would dress like he did when you saw him at the Circle?” said Chelsea and they chuckled.

“Why does this Dorsey fellow interest you? Where was he from?

“Maryland, Hartford County I think. His division, a USCT division, followed three divisions of troops into the aftermath of a huge explosion: a crater dynamited by a mining crew. His second charge secured two-hundred plus prisoners after his first charge planted the Union flag at the back end of this huge circle, but short of Jerusalem Plank Road. Can’t find a word he uttered.”

“Me neither—nary a word!” came a voice from the direction of the doorway.

“Heeeey! We just walked in, grabbed this booth. Chelsea, this in Royce Rice, Mr. jump shot. I call him Ducie.”

"Pleasure is mine, all mine Mrs. Harkness. Figured that Jalen had done well; now I see he has done even better than I could have imagined. It's a pleasure to meet you—may I call you Chelsea?"

"Oh sure—Jalen has told me all about the team, Coach Freeman, your long walks from practices on winter nights—he is especially fond of those *du-wops* you sang on the way home. My husband...."

"Is a helluva guy—my apologies, I interrupted you," said Royce smiling—"who on earth were you talking about?" he continued, adding a tease. Royce wore a gray pinned-striped Hickey Freeman, an understated maroon Countess Mara tie set against a white shirt.

"Sharp," thought Jalen. "Good to see you, mein, and *clean* too," he said.

You took the words right out of my mouth. "Real different from the DuPont Circle description," thought Chelsea.

Royce chuckled, "This is almost like old times; man, a brother has to make a living. But it is a gig I enjoy."

"Oh yeah, we were talking about the old songs, old teachers. Freeman is gone now, bandmaster Cook too—he was related to this guy in the Civil War," said Jalen.

"Yeah—you mentioned—what's his name?"

"Decatur Dorsey," and he waved for the waitress. "I was just telling Chelsea about him. Picture Petersburg, 1864. Grant chasing Lee, nonchalant about a Burnside's plan to blowup Fort Pegram, Meade and Burnside feuding about legacy. Meade suggests to Grant that the agreed upon plan is "impolitic," and convinces him to alter the attack plan already rehearsed by black troops for three or four weeks. Three entire divisions of white troops get bottled up in a disastrous crater of confusion; finally, the black division goes in behind Dorsey. He plants the colors at the other end of the Crater—Cemetery Hill, returns to rally his men and secures Confederate prisoners. For that, he won the Medal of Honor. "I'm looking for the man's words: zip, nothing."

"Still the scrutineer, Needles. You haven't changed a bit since the old days."

"Sorry it took me so long on the drinks; would you folks like to order now? Here's the Pino Grigio for the guys, Cabernet for the lady."

Chelsea ordered broiled trout, Jalen prime rib, Royce rib-eye. Salads arrived all around and variations of veggies included sweet potatoes, sliced tomatoes, sautéed okra, and wild rice.

"Hey man—I wasn't into that history stuff in high school, but in college, had this awesome prof and the light went on! Of course, the Union forces were eventually repelled by a Confederate recovery. But that's enough about me—how in the world did you get started in this undercover stuff?"

"Long story short; military police in Iraq, some college at Maryland, Park Service, metro police—promotion to detective; that history bug bit me too, but nowhere near as deep. But look, let's sing our favorite for your lady. Has she heard it? Your lead or mine?"

"Shu duby, shuby du—shu-duby shuby-du—shu duby, shuby du—shu duby, shuby du...In the still shu-duby shuby du—of the night..." They got a nice round of applause from the customers, near and far.

"Oh man. Those songs got us home safely after many a practice, in deep and dusty snow, and on foot; we may not have been the best team, but we sure could chirp!"

"Doubtless. We weren't the worst either. Say, I ran into Ducie and Richard a few months ago; used to really admire Ducie's quick release, Richard's smooth floater. It's even more a team game now—magnificent players like Magic, LeBron—back in the day everything faced the basket, now it's spin moves, all kinds of dippety-do.'

"That's what year 'round does for you bro, The magicians can play aaalll the positions; crazy! But say, what about you and...."

"Bit the dust two years to the day after graduation; too much time 'way from home. She wanted a castle, I needed a dome, a cave you dig."

"Well hey, I've got a nice friend; next time I can bring her," said Chelsea.

"Folks, how's the food? Now, ain't nobody round that 'preciates old-school more than me. I consider myself a connoisseur of music enterprise. Trouble is, we got entertainment lined up and that last performance puts them at a distinct dis-advantage." The eyes behind the words remained transfixed on Chelsea, though the voice seemed omniscient and the head pivoted. "Solomon Turk at your service—so glad you folks could join us tonight. Please let me know, personally, if you need anything, anything at all!"

XVIII

"Mr. Turk...Solomon, if I may," said Jalen, "I'd like to propose a toast to your establishment!"

"Mister?"

"Harkness, Jalen Harkness—this is my wife Chelsea and my old high school buddy, Royce 'Mr. Jump Shot' Rice, affectionately known over in P.G. as 'Ducie.' We are celebrating a reunion of sorts—haven't hung out for years, and want to toast to old times in the metro mines, toast to retro right here in your place, and take some pictures of our party. Fact is, nobody brought a camera; pardon the imposition, but you can help us if you have one around."

"Should be one right behind the bar. But toast to retro? You must be longtime D.C. Hold on for a minute, let me introduce tonight's entertainment and I'll bring one right over."

"You slipped that in real nice Jalen—almost like Ulysses firing that sweet arching jumper from the corner—long distance," cracked Royce.

"I wish I could have seen you guys play; sounds like you had good camaraderie and the makings of a good team," added Chelsea, her eyes intense as they followed the manuscript of paisley patterns floating against gray pinstripes.

"Chelsea, those were the good old days. D.C. is different, feels different, from the non-drug days. Used to be a time when you couldn't pass a playground without seeing pickup basketball games; where are you from?"

"Ladies and gentlemen. Thank you for your patronage this evening. We are happy to welcome a local trio to our stage tonight. I've seen them perform in a variety of venues, with a variety of instruments. Now this band is unusual, mainly because it sometimes consists of a pickax, conga drum, and washboard—that's right a washboard. Tonight they will start with some a capella love songs, some turn of the century tunes, and some down home blues. Please welcome 'Bottoms Up.'"

"Memphis—grew up there; had relatives here in Maryland, metro D.C., but never much noticed the playgrounds; got started drawing in some weekend classes at the Memphis College of Art. I'm taking some time away from teaching to establish a small studio; pretty tie!"

"Thanks. Yeah, today's D.C. is real different from the town we grew up in; faster pace, glitzier landscape, even the accent is more nasal. Makes me happy seeing Jalen has done well in the wife department. We had some great times. Freeman was a fabulous coach; most guys on the team knew he was special—had an eye for talent, emphasized conditioning and team play. There are very few folks I would grant a holler at the Circle—step to in undercover mode. Dupont Circle was much more reserved, more upscale in the old days than it is now. Who would have thought that drugs, prostitution, espionage would infiltrate, almost define the area as it does now? In our day, I don't think you would see the underside—the rawness that exists there now. Throw in a terrorism threat and you got a real slow burn. Some folks think its the result of the Metro. Jalen *didn't* see the one that I call my 'fudge packer' outfit; I got a bunch of different ones."

"What did you call it—*fudge packer*—that's kinda deep! I think we've got one or two muff munchers around our place but hey, doesn't seem to be a big deal these days. A signal of different times in a different D.C.," commented Jalen.

"We understand that some of tonight's guests have been singing one of our favorite songs; we'd like for you to have a taste of our version of that old favorite, "announced one of the gravediggers.

"You would be surprised at how often I get hit on in a day. But the main thing is that we are there doing the policing that affects drug sales, shoplifting, loitering, robberies, and scans for crazies—terrorists and the like. Hopefully, it keeps that crap minimized. It gets real intense sometimes, but if I had a choice, give me the homo that's got my back, that I can trust; I'd take that any day over a backstabbing hetero—black, blue, green, or fuchsia," said Royce.

"Sounds like you are enjoying your work. Jalen was thrilled to catch up with you, although he was taken aback with, uh, laughed about your outfit. He likes what he's doing too, but lately things have been fairly uphill; he's been kinda focused on trying to get his history students past slavery, to grapple with the freedom push of slaves during the Civil War unit of their American History class."

"Trying to get them to the land of competitive via esteem: laudable. Some of that esteem deficit comes from an intuitive feeling that they can't compete in a quality intellectual way—in the academics. Poor reading is practically inter-generational; grandma, grampa, mom, dad too, mouthing words in silent reading, stumbling when they read out loud. Gangs don't help; churches keep 'em off the streets, but don't always hoist the learning 'jones'. Here's to the Heights—the worth and dignity of each individual, the cocoons of beauty in the arts!"

"Shu-duby, shuby du, Shu-duby, shuby du..." breezed by in close harmony.

"We used to tease you man about being the probe, the scrutineer of the classroom. I always thought that you hated those two dimensional answers, always searching for three dimensions—something you could examine, take apart."

"I caught that bug in Mrs. Hall's history class; always thought she was a really neat teacher—kind of a sophisticated half-smile lurking around the corners of her mouth. Here's to Mrs. Hall."

"You can't imagine the debates we got into on the Civil War; I remember one time we played journalists asking a history author, an author of one of our textbooks, the big questions: who,what , when, why, where. The author was supposedly white. We were in teams and developed questions, all kinds of questions, in rapid fire; wrote 'em down fast as we could think 'em up; asked him questions like—do you believe that African Americans were passive during the war? Passive before the war? After? If turn the other cheek were in vogue, why do wars exist?"

Clapping signaled Bottoms Up finishing their "duby-dus;" they launched into an old blues tune by Solomon Burk called, "Gravedigger's Blues."

"We got caught in a crossfire the other day; kids were just starting to warm up, ask a ton of questions—more than I've heard recently. How many Indian Treaties has the United States broken? Who should ever trust another Treaty? What did they talk and think about? How come black folks disappeared as soon as the war started? Why did all the black folks stay on the plantation or what is a happy darkie? Is there such a thing as a happy pinkie? Why do stupid people need profiles and stereotypes to determine character? How can I keep from getting angry about racial history? What can I do to prevent becoming a sniper or Navy Yard attacker—learn to navigate tense situations. What is the history of race riots—slave rebellions? Or, if justice were fair, how many white folk would have to be slaughtered to make up for blacks lost in the slave trade? If black folk refused to leave the plantation, where did the ones joining the army come from? We had fun coming up with those, but behind each question were two senses—desperation and provocation."

"Oh yeah, of course! They wanted to see how *you* engage that shit, and they are desperate for answers for themselves. I had those questions about everything; you too. My answer has been to celebrate the shepherds! But hey, come to think of it, I think I saw something about that—you guys, your tour at the Douglass Mansion in the paper. Saw those kids, your kids, spread-eagled all over the lawn. "

> *"We be the gravedigger's three, uh-huh, uh huh,*
> *Buried both rebs and yankees...uh-huh, uh huh,*

"Yeah, we all had to duck—hug the ground when we heard shots fired. The kids listened sharply and, believe it or not, actually *listened*—performed with *exactitude*."

"It's a miracle no one was hurt," said Chelsea; she sketched the scene on her napkin as she peered into her mind's eye.

> *"We wuz always on hand to cover bodies with land,*
> *Way fore there wuz Martin or the Klu Krooked Klan."*

"Dude, I saw a photo and that article in the Afro-News—guess they got there a bit after all the excitement. Anyway, they had photos of the students about to board a bus; you could see *two* buses in the photo.

Sounded like some of them were really shook up—there was this one girl, kinda heavy set, pulling a trash can upright."

"Jalen, did you see that one? Sounds like it may have been your Tofu?"

"Oh yeah; Dennison hit me over the head with it as soon as I walked into school; I think that's the same one your parents saw. How's your trout honey? Sure smells good from here."

"We wuz always on hand to cover bodies with land,"

"For the most part, they generally have good cooks here. Those three are short order fill-ins from time to time, handy men, henchmen, gravediggers—you name it and they've probably done it."

"Trying to get these kids in touch with that focused patience of their forebearers; nowadays, everyone of them seems pissed off about something; on the edge of fisticuffs and gangs. Never seen Turk at a parents meeting, so he wouldn't know that his daughter is in my class. Mother shows up when there is an emergency. I saw those same dudes digging a hole at Ebenezer Hill just the other day. Do they work for Turk?"

"Way fore there wuz Martin or the Klu Krooked Klan."

"Sometimes. I've seem them up at the Circle a time or two."

"Jalen, how's your steak?" said Chelsea.

"Tasty." On the last chew, before washing it down with a small swallow, he choked on the morsel that was caught in his throat. *Damn man, you can't swallow and talk at the same time.* Closing the outside door behind her and moving towards the kitchen was Tofu Turk; she spotted him and closed the space between herself and their table.

"Hi, Mr. Harkness."

"Tofu—good to see you. We were just talking about the picture you took; Royce here saw one of you pulling up a trash can."

"Yeah–it reminded me of the one I crashed into at school, but I did more than touch that one. I came over here to get some carry-out for dinner. Wanted to come over before they ran out of catfish and before the ghosts come out." Clapping overrode her obvious respect for the ancients spirits.

"Tofu, you remember Chelsea from class, and my good friend Royce. Royce, Tofu. Did you say ghosts—did you walk through the cemetery?"

"Oh yeah; they know me by name by now—we have both black and white, rebs and yankees buried right there in Eb'nezer Hill. They likes to talk almost as much as you do—got some weird stories to tell. Mostly, I jus' listen. They gets along real well—watch over me when those gang folks want to jack me up. Those Apotres get real nervous when I duck into the cemetery. Got me some tin cans—smaller than the one I bumped into that I bang while I hoot. If I talk in school, they'd know it was me a-hootin'. It makes 'em really run; puts them in a wicked scare. Better scoot, thanks for the marshmallows Ms. Harkness."

"Tofu, do you know these people?"

"Yes Daddy, this is my teacher at school, Mr. Harkness and his wife and a friend of theirs."

"Well—Mr. Hark—ness! Tofu, your package is at the carry-out window. Harkness huh—you folks at the school can't seem to stop putting students in screwed-up positions; crashing into trash cans, embarrassing themselves trying to read, and now getting shot at. You think you are lifting them up and around every corner comes a new problem; I'm beginning to think you folks don't have the foggiest idea of what you are doing! You want me to toast to that? Next you're going to tell me y'all are going to that reenactment down at Petersburg for the Crater."

"First of all Solomon, I'm almost sure that we can straighten out whatever reading difficulty Tofu has, once we get it fully diagnosed. Secondly, that incident at the Douglass Mansion was just pure bad luck; we were fortunate since no one was hurt. And yes, I am headed to the Crater reenactment but *without* students. They have completed their portion of the tour. This is a development opportunity for me. I hope to write an article about it; an article on Decatur Dorsey."

"Bully for you! Glad to know that you're looking to be better informed. They got lots of black 'Peters' lodged down there in that crater. I'll hope to be there on the Confederate side helping to make sure that you yanks don't miss your education. By the way, somebody moved that camera. Enjoy!"

XIX

Street lights had blossomed forth capturing pools of steam levitating above hot asphalt. Vaporous clouds of steam glided, settling around lower portions of Ebenezer hill, embellishing it in cotton-like fringes. Though blurred, a path through the cemetery was the shortest route to her barn-house; she relished her solitary walks there, in contrast to common predilections. *Is that place haunted? Are witches and goblins up in there?* Those were questions her mates in school asked when they watched her take the ghostly path. "Yeah, and they will happily seize your *ass* if you mess with me!" She had been in her dad's tavern only ten minutes. She pulled up her hood. *We know where you live bitch; fuck-up your orders and you'll fry like a chicken wing in your daddy's tavern.*

During daylight, she could see scraps of old newspapers, plastic grocery bags, beer cans and motley, yellowed condoms strewn about with other more common litter: calcified dog-shit, abandoned birds nests, pieces of wet cardboard. The outer perimeter of the entrance to the path captured windblown detritus, the inner reaches showed the trash of the brave and more adventurous. She considered the halfway point, the point between the tavern and her house, her private sanctuary—a hiding place; *There I can think, escape from Queen Esther's nagging mouth, and talk with ancient spirits.*

She hadn't always been a hoodie; but experience taught her that the hood protected her voice. She'd mumbled that "happily seize you" line once with those Apostles, those Apôtres of Chienne. It worked for a while, but was later challenged when they'd taunted her as a group, encircled her and threatened to lob fire-bombs, from the cemetery into her bedroom window. Experience also taught her that as individuals, they were afraid to follow her into the cemetery. *Glad I bought that bucket.* The bucket was a miniature version of the trash can; it held twelve quarts and was made by Behrens. That name was on the trash can, too. She tied it to a long string; one end on bucket, the other to a empty can. *Just howl like an owl or ghost.*

We be the gravedigger's three, uh-huh, uh huh,

The small can was in her bedroom. She felt herself levitate when she practiced some spells and chants she'd memorized from the verses of Hoodoo and sorcery contained in the few books held in her house, the ones in her mother's séance office. *I got those markers memorized too— Williams, Westbrook, Proctor, Hamilton.* The path she'd worn through the cemetery was dotted with surnames similar to those of students she attended school with everyday.

Buried both rebs and yankees...uh-huh, uh huh,

It's kinda cold out here. Didn't seem that cold when I walked over, but it's colder now? The iron collar keys jangled in her pants pocket as she walked; she slowed, looked over her shoulder, saw one of the Apostles glaring, standing at the rim of the cemetery; *following me!* Tofu gripped the catfish she'd bought with both hands; one of the waist-high bushes might knock the brown bag out of her hands. Or she might slip and have no free hand to break a fall; *or swing a stick.* She bent over in mid-stride, picked up a sturdy straight branch selected by a wide glance she'd thrown into the darkened, misty glades.

Hmmmm, that fish sure smells good. Wonder why Mr. Jalen was in daddy's restaurant tonight? There with his wife too; she seems nice, like she was

131

having a good time. Wonder if they have a library like the one at school at their house? There with his buddy, the one that was at DuPont Circle that day, all dressed up like a woman. Apostles had a field day wid dat one—talked about Mr. Jalen real bad, said he was really on the down low. Bitches gossip about anything. Shouldn't a let 'em make me jump on dat goil in the cafeteria. Shit, she had it coming to 'er. Damn Damisi slid dat tray right unner my ass—real quick—felt like I was a bullet headed for the trash can, happened so fast. Gotta be crazy, but the speed felt real good—'cept for the crash into the can—slop, banana peels, clumps of bread, all sorts of other crap. A series of quivers shuddered her spine; her trap was set, the bucket was lidded and hidden behind a stone marker. Beneath it lay an iron collar, *just like the one mom puts on me.*

We know where you live lil' yella bitch and you had better not forget your orders. The words choked her neck, crowbarred her considerable emotional fortress, played its mean melody on her spine. Her shoulders shivered and shook. *It ain't my fault I was born this color, almost the color of tofu, half tan, half white—wasn't none of my doin'. I love daddy even if he is white; now mom, the judge told me where I got to live.* Frazzled by her own appearance, the questioning looks that passersby gave her, she gloried when asked, "Your daddy owns that tavern up by Ebenezer Hill, don't he?"

I hate counselor Dennison even more—hate her smell, her blotchy skin, her prissy demeanor, musty odor—like she pisses on herself. Tofu gagged when Dennison came over to the house—*to share literacy with the great unwashed.* "You ain't half as dumb as you pretend to be Tofu. Now work on this software and write down your scores after you get through. Each time, you should get a little better score, dearie; I've got to get downstairs to my séance sos I can contact my long lost relatives. They gone tell me 'bout my next steps." The woman treated her sessions like many treat religion; *maybe magic is religion—religion magic?* Tofu looked backwards again; *gone.* She took a deep breath thinking, "One day one of them bitches gon' come in—one day." *My trap is ready.*

On occasion, when the woman had come over during the summer months, Tofu had avoided her by waiting on the peak of her pathway, performing a little séance of her own. Her mom had strictly forbidden her to "play with herself." But she found that the onset of puberty—the time her mom said girls become women, caused strange, but enjoyable sensations in her "self"—in what some of the other girls called their "Cherry," or "Mimi." She couldn't see the semi-glaze in her eyes, the flushed reddening of her cheeks and shoulders, but she glowed in the subsequent physical eruption—it left her relaxed and liberated—free of anxiety and angry annoyances (caused by whatever circumstance had triggered it in the first place). Her reading scores had improved ever so slightly, but her ability to talk, to speak in front of adults, had diminished remarkably. In fact, she found herself almost stupefied when asked to read aloud. That's when the ghosts had started to speak with her on the pathway—especially if she were there at night. *Have the ghosts stolen my voice?*

Buried both rebs and yankees...uh-huh, uh huh,

"Folks 'round here don't believe dat slaves is buried right here in 'Neezer Hill. Yeah, um tellin' you truthful child, right neath that wide-ass bum a yourns. Talking 'bout black folk ain't neber been fightin' for dere own freedom. Had to fight to git *in* de fight—den had to fight rebs, den had to fight agin once de fight was over—been fightin' ever since. But can't none a ya'll see it. Shit, been watchin' yall gits terrorized de whole time. Started wid de chains, den came de laws, den the whippin's got worser and worser. Nobody believes sum of da stories dese here ghosts gots to tell. An they *still* don' want ch'all to gits educated—git something in your head. And now y'all don' gone *RETRO!* Gold dis, gold dat— chains, tattoos, spikes in your mouth. Hell, you might as well go on and put a iron jail around your heads. How you think you gon' compete in the workplace? 'Bois don' said it time and time again, read and cipher, cipher and read. Musta neber *seen* the iron jail—de head lock dey puts on my Jacob. Had to wear dat heavy piece of shit for weeks. And dese gangs—now dat ain't nuttin' new. From dese dummies, you take orders; orders ain't nuttin' but answers, no questions allowed. You don't get to ask those. Turn any pack a folks loose widout training and dats what cho gits—a pack a *dawgs. You gots to scare the shit outta dem 'postles; bring 'em in here to us!"* Tofu tightened the drawstring on her hood.

Another ghost chimed in, "You brung us some catfish?—we can't use dat! Read to us from your schoolbooks. Teach us to read; use dat walkie talkie you gots setup. You can read to us right from your bedroom!!" She couldn't; not a word would come out. "Oh yeah girlfriend—I seen slayberry from head to toe, shor' to shor'. You best be believin' ain't nobody gon' make sure you gits your education but your *self.* Hell. The best part of being a ghost is dat you gits to fly, gits to see and not be seen. I seen segregated school houses all over de land—wooden ones on stilts in Memphis, quonset huts in Alabama, *behind* outhouses in the red clay of Macon. I be blessed wid de lossa sens' of smell—buzzards wouldn't get caught in suma dose places. Learnin' starts right in your own head— luckily wid yo parents, but hell we didn't have none a dem for de mos' part. Rebs make sure they wuz workin' double duty, sos dey don' have energy or time for dey own." Sometimes the racket overwhelmed her and she started running for the end of the path, other days she just whistled loudly to drown the poor devils out—especially when they started talking to her during the daylight hours.

Nobody had to bet her if slaves, former slaves, freed and Jim-Crowed black folk, were in that cemetery. They spoke to her *all* the time. If slaves were there, then—*I know damn well one or some of them were soldiers.* Tofu shivered, brushed dampness from her sweat jacket, clutched the damp bag harder, and swung her stick against a tree. "Shut up!" she shouted. Now the apostles were after her too—she had tried appeasement, taking small requests and performed them dutifully—*carry my tray, scratch my back, give me your homework.* The more she complied, the more insistent the demands became; *is mom part of the conspiracy?* She'd even used that old slave chain in the attic—the one that came down from her great, great, granddaddy—to punish her for *backtalk. Rusty piece of shit! Hope she doesn't miss the second one.* The hood and the earplugs helped; *and no one gets to hear my voice except these ghosts, gets to know where it comes from, or how it sounds, unless they are trapped in my cemetery.*

She halted as she came near the house—*uh-oh, that 's Dennison's car*—and lurked out of sight behind the last oak tree before a small clearing. She watched as her mom kissed Dennison full-mouthed, exchanged a word or two, waved and closed the door. She waited until Dennison cranked the engine, waited until the Cadillac the woman had spent every nickel, dime and quarter on, lurched backwards. She waited until—*that bitch*—turned on her lights, and then she waited some more. After five minutes, she lunged against the door breathless and pounded, pummeled it until Queen Esther answered, terrified and heaving around the chest.

"Whew, I ran all the way!" said Tofu breathing hard. "I think there were some Gothic ghosts and shit after me."

XX

"I'll drive, be the designated driver, freight the weight. I enjoyed meeting Royce—it's wonderful that you guys can get together, spend some time getting reacquainted;" *plus you had one or two drinks extra in case we get stopped*. I guess I'm jealous in a way—it's nice being close enough to home turf to hook up with old high school friends. What's going to happen at the reenactment?" Chelsea said, after cranking the car, steering it towards Connecticut Avenue.

"Well that's a good question. Tell you the truth, I'm not sure myself. I found that old civil war jacket. I suppose they'll have a lecture or two, a tour, maybe even a walk through of some of the events that happened, perhaps a movie. I've done a ton of reading about the battle at the Crater. Got a pretty good idea of the order of battle, some background stuff about the troops involved, the military essentials. Did some reading on the reviews and inquiries put together after the battle; read some on the battle at Fort Pillow also. Both battles were controversial. For sure, it's fascinating to compare those reviews—almost like a metaphysical comparison of the attitudes towards black soldiers among the military brass—Congress too."

"I enjoyed being in the classroom today; kinda fun. I hope their reactions to my painting are good. Let me see those sometime—maybe when you get back—don't want to jinx myself. Matter of fact, I had an inspiration right in the restaurant. I jotted it down on a napkin," said Chelsea.

"You mean about the class?"

"Uh-huh. Noticed a small keloid on Tofu's ankle, just below a tattoo. I made some sketches of an idea that came to me. I'll show it to you."

"Great."

The melding of their comparative psyches had fostered a strong respect between them for one another's talents, though their individual spirits had taken them in different directions with regard to their teaching careers. Chelsea had decided to take some time off away from teaching—a break from the rigors and stresses of the drills and finger-paintings of middle school munch-kins. The pieces she had created in her spare time—"Slavery Eviscerated," "Ignorance Unblemished," "After Mirth," had sold quickly, fueling her belief that she could match her teaching salary and establish an art studio in the mother-in-law attachment of their home. "After-Mirth," done in a colorful cubist style, pictured a group of slaves, scared with keloids, yet rapturous in the announcement of the Emancipation Proclamation. The foreground sported the joyous freed slaves, the middle ground instruments of torture and enslavement and the background, leaves of tobacco and balls of cotton. Her largest payment came from a work entitled "Retro-Psyche."

"Jalen, this is perfect—totally perfect. Look at the windows—almost like the library at Monticello, windows in the round." And it allowed the fluent flow of light into the small room. "It's soo beautiful—I could almost paint the ceiling—become my own Michelangelo."

Chelsea had loved the Chesapeake Bay style cottage they'd found with an adjacent "mother-in-law" wing built in the round; "My rotunda," she called it. It was a better choice than the barn-house that disappeared from the market in only a week. They both shared an interest in the history of the black experience; for him it was the travel backwards in time to spear the thinking, stratagems and kaleidescope of emotions that sparkled in their ancestor's minds. For Chelsea, it was the leap forward, winged by the aesthetic of African American culture, which fueled her creativity.

"The oranges, coppers, reds, maroons and deep purples of the skin—the variations in muscle, rhythm, and facial features, hon'," she said, is what arrested her attention, inspired her creations. "Just check out the geometry of the sculptures, Jalen."

"You remember what you asked me when we first met?" said Jalen.

"Of course I remember; I was so pitifully shy."

"Hey—that was *not* a question a shy woman asks."

"It is for me, and embarrassing when I think about it now."

"Really?"

"Really. There was just no other way. I needed a male model and was desperate. You seemed like a nice enough guy and you were—are, handsome and well-built. I took a chance—calculated, since we were in that class together. Seeing you like that in the Florida Avenue market, I thought—'take a chance.'"

"Lemme show you a short cut—make a left here babe."

She flashed blinkers for the left, slowed for the car in front. "I do love making things with my hands, the joy of creation, especially the end product—something I can step back and look at."

"I have to admit that you were right about the natural light in your studio—really glorious."

Light swam, frolicked and chattered in "Retro-Psyche." The chiaroscuro study compared teeming mentalities of contemporary African-American youngsters, laden with the aspects of slavery in their minds; sex with bondage, whips for spankings, collars for every limb of the body, chains for controlling the mind. "I was looking for a way far-out blacks imitate the ethic of selected whites, the Goths with their Gothic ethos seemed a perfect parallel."

"When these black kids go beyond slavery to Gothic, then you can watch out for real."

They got out of the car and once home, settled in the studio and left it dark.

"Lemme fix you a drink—I'll water mine down a bit," said Jalen, adding "Thanks for taking that class invitation so well and being a good sport." He made a rum and coke for her and a vodka Collins for himself. A panorama of lights in the dense neighborhood shone before them. "I love being close to you Chelsea, love my "Rotunda moma," and they enjoyed a long, warm kiss. "It was great to see Royce tonight, reminisce about old times. Those gravediggers were surprisingly good."

"Uh-huh, uh huh," giggled Chelsea, pointing at the carnival of lights flickering in the darkness and kicking off her shoes. "He was glad to see you too—be sure to save his card so we can get in touch with him. Ummmm, this is good. Jalen, there is sadness in Tofu's eyes."

"I see that too—some sort of retro-psyche—I like that term."

"Me too. From where I sit sometimes black folk get trapped into chasing the white dream—the provincial one—the one that falls short of continental. You know the one—where you grab all the space, all the money, all the power you can. Hemingway bravura for the men, Marilyn

Monroe style pussycat for the women—pure bitch underneath a fuzzy coat. Ain't really anything new—we had to get back-stabbed in Africa to get here—by some of our own brothers and sisters. Black, white, blue, green or yellow, the concept of team escapes us on a daily basis. It took a sense of team to survive slavery, the ability to plot, plan, strategize—form a cohesive team. Old black couples that laugh and smile together; they have that. They learned how to build creative teams.

Yeah—I know what you mean. My parents had that—yours too. Saw them take out a plain piece of paper, huddled together, and map out a budget, write out priorities."

"Your minister had us do that dialogue journal—part of our counseling—you remember that?"

"Yeppy...I do."

"I hid a cigarette—could do with one right about now—mind if I light it?"

"No hon', go ahead. But only one."

The flint of the struck match exploded, flamed into a momentary sear of orange and red; flushing the domed ceiling. "That's what happened at the Crater. The image was inverted," he said surveying the ceiling, "the dome was instead a huge, flaming *bowl*." He drew a shallow inhale and offered a drag to Chelsea.

"Thanks," she said and pulled him closer to her with his necktie. "Feels like you have more to tell me. Why don't we just snuggle closer, so we can talk about those wonderful little chestnuts you use to spark my rotunda-shaped spirits."

"Aha—lil' sista "C" be on the prowl—good to know that she still thinks about old mister "T" and his sidekicks. The city lights are really beautiful tonight. Look at all those lights flickering and tinkering all over the place, flitting about like little fireflies." Chelsea kissed him on the neck as he massaged her thigh.

"Fireflies in the fall?"

"Hey—fireflies whenever. Especially when I am this close to you. Snuggle, snuggle," he quipped, "nature is in de house."

"You're nuts, ha ha," she said.

"That too. From my perspective it beats the alternative. I see that vein in your forehead—it twinkles with the stars and rises when you are excited. Why don't you mention it when lil' sis tears up, moistens?"

"Why don't you speak up when one-eyed Jalen wants to jump the fence." They kissed and nuzzled. Thirst for oneness flooded the small, round room, cleansed it of distractions, reinforced and saddled itself in the stirrups that ignited the gallop in their attraction.

"I always love the scent of your skin, its lovely texture."

"I love the arch of you inside me, and since you put a question to me, let me sail one to you. Where is that wonderful package that you promised me when we married...huh?"

The shared laughter, shared kisses and frivolous tickles; Jalen dropped to his knees and by her buttocks, pulled her legs around him, pulled her body to the edge of the small foot high love-seat. Her opened skirt fell off seamlessly; the feel of her skin, bared within her dress surprised him. "Where is your bra, your panties?"

"I'll never tell."

He felt the glisten shield him from friction, measuredthe distance in miles of travel with each felt millimeter, and relished the presence of her around him. *It's amazing when psychic and physical joy erupts at the same moment.* It was a moment that brought his soul to its knees in prayer. *Yes indeed baby*; "I love me some Chelsea, yes indeed."

"Uhhhh-huh!!"

XXI

"I'm off Chelsea—left some toast, an egg and oatmeal for you in the kitchen. I'll call you from the road."

"Wait baby, can I change my mind? I'm gonna miss you; gotta stop sleeping so soundly. I wanted to make you a good breakfast. Be sure to call me, especially when you get settled, let me know how you like it."

"Will do, and too late sugar, my mind is already on the road, body got a foot in the gas tank. I'm back—nine or ten-ish tomorrow night."

Jalen poured himself an extra cup of coffee, rolled one egg into his toast, grabbed his duffel bag and blue uniform and revved the engine in her 2001 Subaru. He double-checked his bags for his camera and smartphone, put on the red sun-glasses given him by Spence. The route that he had chosen took him across the Sousa bridge and down Interstate two ninety-five. He glanced in the direction of the old Watergate barge, where the military bands gave concerts in the shadow of the Lincoln Memorial and asked himself one question: *what do I know about Decatur Dorsey?* "I know he married after the war—married Mannie Christie. I know he died in July, 1891 in Hoboken, New Jersey. I know he was discharged from Union army on the 4th of Dec., 1865. I know that he died from rheumatic fever caused from malaria and typhoid, probably contracted during his military service. And, I know that he signed his own name; he could write and read," thought Jalen, tapping the steering wheel with each point. *Wonder if the reason he never wrote his memoirs or a narrative of his experiences was because of the painful effects of rheumatoid arthritis.* I also know that the 1890 census taken in Baltimore showed several Dorseys: Charles, James H., James W., Joseph, and Moses.

He noted signs for Lorton, then Chancellorsville; afterwards, his thoughts drifted, divided between the sights and sounds of traffic, the markers showing lessening distance to Richmond. For a moment, he considered the newly developed rapport between Damisi and Tofu. Girl stepped right up to the challenge at Harpers Ferry—she tried. He put his speed on cruise control, reflected on the tour that he'd shared with his class, and took in the Richmond landscape, reached at slightly less than two hours. *Took the Union four years.* He flexed his bladder as he passed Richmond, realizing too late that he needed to make a pee stop. Before him loomed the Varina-Enon Bridge. The beautiful structure spanning the James River southeast of Richmond sported inverted "Vs" on its harp-like cable. As he cast glancing looks into the James River, he imagined the challenge between the two girls...no, Burnside and Meade, in a logrolling competition, both frantically running fore and aft, attempting to dislodge the other. The image, framed atop a floating trash can, brought a big smile to his face. *Wonder if they can form a team?* He smiled on the image and grinned at the thought of his nickname: *Needles. Can you puncture the riddle of Decatur Dorsey—no pics, no words, only a tombstone.*

After crossing the bridge, he stopped to relieve himself and briefly looked at the notes he'd brought along that offered perspectives on the Battle of the Crater Buried deep in his mind were highlighted notes, a quote from Shakespeare's Hamlet:

I am thy father's spirit, Doom'd for a certain term to walk the night, And for the day confined to fast in fires, till the foul crimes done in my days of nature
    Are burnt and purged away. But that I am forbid to tell the secrets of my prison-house, I could a tale unfold whose lightest word would harrow up thy

soul, freeze thy young blood, Make thy two eyes, like stars, start from their spheres, thy knotted and combined locks to part And each particular hair to stand on end, like quills upon the fretful porcupine: But this eternal blazon must not be to ears of flesh and blood. List, list, O, list! If thou didst ever thy dear father love...

He wore the sunglasses found at the Lincoln Memorial for the balance of the ride from the bridge to Petersburg. Jalen reflected on the father's ghosted spirit as the collective spirit of African-American fighters during the great contest of 1862 called the American Civil War. They had disciplined their rebuke of slavery towards fighting for freedom and the Union, spirited afterwards in the Great World Wars, and additionally in the fight for Civil Rights. He arrived in Petersburg a little after twelve and headed towards his motel. Upon securing his motel room, he drove to the site of the reenactment just in time to witness the lighting of a huge bonfire. The tour guide beckoned him towards the fire, and he joined a collection of men, women, boys and girls there to take part in the reenactment.

"Thank you," he said to the assistant passing out maps of troop movements during the battle. He fish-eyed the scene thinking, *gosh, there are a lot more folks here than I thought would attend,* before moving his ears back to the guide. Behind the handsome figure of the female guide, a flock of geese, frightened by the ringing fire of battlefield armaments, lifted like pages of Tofu's dossier, into the air. Their elongated bodies mounted sundry breezes like fading jet-streams. The barks of the rifles made a music in sharp contrast to the lyrical magic of Dennison's keys. He wondered if the key to dialog between feuding parties was locked away in a file cabinet somewhere. The tan uniform of the guide fitted her nicely and curved to accentuate her legs and well sculpted buttocks. Most winning about her was the clean, lucid, transparency of her brown eyes. Her focused rapport with listeners was assisted by a broad smile and efficient gestures. He hoisted his sunglasses and returned her gaze. "The eyes *can be* windows to the soul."

145

"You will be assigned to troops that participated in the battle by lottery and choice. If you want to be assigned by choice, wear your uniform if you brought one, if by lottery, put your name in this bucket," she announced.

"An accommodation to diversity," he thought. *Good.*

"We have put the various stages of the battle on transparencies so that you are able to follow these events in terms of the strongest nests of fire. The approximate times of events will be on the maps. Be sure to bring them with you in the morning, as we will refer to them during the opening session. For your information, we will have a noted historian talk abut the context of the battle in the morning and study the battle in retrograde tomorrow afternoon. Now, take a moment to smell the bonfire that we have built for you—straw, limestone, dried mud, wooden logs, sulfur—these are the smells that greeted the troops on both sides of this battle minus the smell of human flesh. Stop to listen beyond your own footfalls, peel back layers of time, and you can hear the yells of surprised Confederates, the sizzle of flesh, watch the orbit of fissioned limbs, see the smoke and arc of furious flames—hear the rumble of explosives foment beneath the earth. This, followed by the supreme climatic moment when hell meets the dark morning sky and licks its cloudy cheeks with a mighty fury. Here are Burnside's orders for the battle:"

"1. The T-shaped mine, built by Colonel Pleasants under Fort Pegram, was to be exploded at 3:30 am
2. General Ledlie was to move his troops forward, the object being Cemetery Hill.
3. General Willcox was to move forward bearing to the left to protect the flank of Ledlie's troops.
4. General Potter was to move his troops forward, bearing to the right to protect the right flank of Ledlie's troops. The object of both flanking

troops was Jerusalem Plank Road on the left, the ravine fronting the Confederate main line on the right.

5. General Ferrero was to advance beyond both troops their object being a village to the right."

"As many of you already know, neither Ferrero or Ledlie went into the Crater with their troops. They are documented to have been sharing decanters of *rum* in a surgeon's bombproof at the time their troops entered battle. Their troops became hopelessly entangled in bombproofs, trenches and debris, and it is thought that they had little idea of their military objectives. The colored troops, contemporaneously called blacks, went in last and suffered extraordinary mauling, but with significant accomplishment."

"The maps that we are passing out to you represent the troop movements at various times of the battle. More specifically, the times are as follows: 4:44—the time when the explosion took place, creating a crater 170 feet by 80 and 20 feet deep; 8:00—the time when black troops when into the Crater; the time when when the battle became a stalemate, and 1:00—the time when the battle becomes a desperate struggle of fists, bayonets, and rifle butts. Notice that the time of the explosion occurs much later than the planned time of 3:30 am. This is because the charge had to be re-ignited, as the initial fuse went out and required re-lighting. So, tomorrow we will meet at 9:00 am for a study of the context in which the battle was fought. I understand that our guest may also include a comparative portion devoted to the congressional reviews of both Fort Pillow and The Crater. And last but not least, you will receive the battle groups to which either you choose or are assigned. Thereafter, we will break for lunch and we will do a slow motion walk through of the "Battle of the Crater" which includes a brief discussion of the way the tunnel was constructed. Are there any questions?"

"Are women or whites allowed—encouraged—to participate as members of the USCT?"

"The answer to both your questions is yes. That way we feel that you can experience the conditions of hatred and animus felt towards the black troops as they fought for their freedom as newly minted soldiers in the Union army. Theirs was a mantra of 'Remember Fort Pillow.'"

"Other questions?"

"You mean the Fort Pillow Massacre?"

"Yes. The fate of the garrison at Fort Pillow echoed throughout both the media and armies of the day. There were congressional reviews of both the Crater and Fort Pillow. Statistical abstracts of the events at Fort Pillow suggests severe retribution against black soldiers by Confederate troops."

"Other questions?"

"Good. Then we will see you in the morning. Adios."

Jalen was impressed by the delivery and professionalism of the tour guides. He secured his maps, made a quick stop for salad and fried chicken, retired to his motel room, and called Chelsea. "Baby, all good on this end—how did things go?"

"Hey sweetheart—we had a fabulous time. I got some good work done."

"Awesome. I am kinda tired, so I'm gonna call it a day."

"Okay. Take plenty of pictures and call me when you can."

"Gotcha—will do. Love from Petersburg babe."

"Ha ha...you better mean that," said Chelsea.

The next morning, Jalen joined the reenactors on the battlefield premises for a lecture from a distinguished Civil War historian. "The military man, desperate to live, is like the great artist; he engages experience at the peak of all his senses," droned the esteemed historian, his voice craggy-edged, designed to pierce the wind, rain, and range of large battlefields. "It is believed by many that the *ears* of the great Ulysses S. Grant were not present and engaged during the 'Battle of the Crater.' Neither were those of lesser generals Ambrose Burnside and George Meade; in order for Burnside to update Meade on the progress of the battle. Burnside was a significant distance from the battle theater, so as to correspond with Meade by telegraph. Like the finely attuned ears of the symphonic concertgoer, Grant could visualize in his minds-eye, the sounds of varied canon, small arms fire, musketry, pistol fire, and the positions of the troops—the nests of furious encounters, the concentrations of arms and voices—literally the shape of the battle—from the *sounds* of its instruments. He had demonstrated this gift, particularly at Forts Donelson and Henry. Burnside and Meade entertained great animosity towards one another grounded in Burnside's having to report to Meade, his superior officer, subsequent to Burnside's embarrassing loss at Chancellorsville and Meade's great victory at Gettysburg."

"Lincoln, at this point in his presidency, was up for reelection, and feared that he would lose and lose badly, if the country were not presented with some hopeful sign that the Union effort was achieving its war objectives. Lincoln needed another victory in his march to end the war. In his campaign to subvert the Confederate effort—rob it of its labor force and property—and use the labor and energy of slaves in the Confederacy, he had issued the Emancipation Proclamation, freeing the slaves and urging military engagement on the part slaves, male and female. Troops of black males were called United States Colored Troops and were significantly engaged in Grants' campaign in the east and west, as he was now the supreme military commander."

In his own mind's eye, Jalen could almost see the silhouetted figure of Decatur Dorsey, slim of build, sleek in movement, slight of stature, sail past the carnage of the renowned blast on his way to Cemetery Hill to plant the colors of USCT 39th on that hill. *What about Decatur Dorsey—that man earned a Medal of Honor during this battle—how on earth did he do it?* Jalen's attention was momentarily distracted by the melodious sounds of an ice-cream truck sporting popsicles and funnel cakes up on Jerusalem Plank Road.

XXII

"It is significant to understand that the Union lost 3,798 casualties 200 wounded and 1500 captured in this battle. On the Confederate side, 361 killed, 727 wounded, and 403 captured. So we count this as a Confederate victory. Meade had altered Burnside's arrangements for a tunnel, proposed by Colonel Henry Pleasants and a regiment of coal miners from Pennsylvania. Burnside wanted 10,000 pounds of gunpowder for a mine to be dug under Fort Pegram with the aim of blowing it up. Meade had that poundage reduced to 8,000 pounds. The corps of engineers engaged at the battle theater, felt that the development of the tunnel was impossible due to its length and the impossibility of proper ventilation; however, the Pennsylvania coal miners used their experience with fire and flamed ventilation methods to pragmatically refute this claim."

"Of course Burnside is pissed about all of this. He has already given Ferrero the task of training the USCT 39th to lead the charge into the breach of the explosion and responds to Meade's subsequent and subsidiary concerns in detail. Meade not only holds his ground on those issues, but prior to that concern, proposes that the order of battle be changed. Ostensibly, this is due to Lincoln's upcoming elect-..."

"Bang!" the explosion of several high flying balloons startled the ears of the listeners, the group having grown significantly since the lecture's beginning. Babies, very young children, teen-agers and a few blacks here and there now made up a larger crowd.

"...election. In the point of view of other historians, I might add, who feel that Meade's decision to reject having the blacks enter the breach at first and have them enter last, this was further example of his documented prejudice towards blacks. Additionally, he was unclear in his battle orders for Ledlie's troops, who were unclear about their objectives once in the crater.

"Common enough," thought Jalen, as he swatted a group of persistent gnats swarming his immediate area, determined not to be an obvious scrutineer.

"Grant doubted the propriety of challenging the commanding general and sided with Meade, thus relegating Ferrero's troops—now thoroughly trained for their sprint to Cemetery Hill and their ultimate objective of Jerusalem Plank Road—to be the *last* of four divisions to enter the Crater. I should add that Ledlie's troops went into the crater without gambions, footbridges, hatchets, ladders—in short, without assault implements. They also had no clear orders on a method of retreat."

God! In a brief fantasy, he revisited his driving fantasy—*Burnside and Meade, balancing their upright bodies like lumberjacks, logrolling on the James River in a contest to see which one would fall in first.*

"The divisions of Ledlie, Willcox, and Potter enter into the breach of the crater and are therein trapped—remember this crater is 20 to 30 feet deep and festooned with bombproofs and abatis, designed to prevent the advance of enemy troops. Abatis was used much like barbed-wire fencing is used today. As the battle wore on, they loomed as fish in a barrel—ready targets for the musketry, sabers, and rifle-butts of Confederate soldiers, now reviving after the initial explosion. We will stop here; you are to receive your re-enactment assignments and gather here at 1:00 for the reenactment—which will be in slow motion, with actors preassigned to your units; they will pantomime the events of that egregious battle in miniature as you accompany them. Your tour guide will assist you at that time. Are there any questions?"

"Yes," he thought in silence, "what did Dorsey say about his brigade? Did he say anything about how he won that Medal of Honor, about how Siegfried managed to maneuver his troops to Cemetery Hill?About how he planted that Union flag on the hill in the midst of all that chaos?" He tried to raise his hand but it remained at his side, limp, lifeless. In the midst of the crowd, he felt embarrassed; *your fore-bearers fought and died right here, on this very soil—and you can't even raise your hand to ask a god-damned question—piece of shit—garbage!*

During the lunch break, he visited the burial grounds at Petersburg— walked around noting the names of those who died in that conflict. He had no flowers with which to honor their graves, no mementos to leave to show his appreciation for their work he enjoyed during his lifetime. *Surely his mere presence was not enough. Here I am strolling through Poplar Grove Cemetery—Weaver, Brown, Porter, Stewart, all dead for the cause of humanity, and I cannot raise my hand.*

"Once you have located your flag," said the female tour guide, "ladies and gentlemen, line up as best you can; your company leaders will help you get organized. Raise your hand if you have no idea where you should be...obviously, Confederates should be with gray flags and Federals with blue ones."

Smiles and giggles met that comment; a general frenzy ensued with a sprightly white gentleman lining up right behind him.

"Wesley Whitworth here, you are?

Jalen—Jalen Harkness. Pleased to meet cha."

153

"Pleasure. Guess you're wondering why I want to be with the coloreds. My ancestors owned slaves—thought I'd come up and pay my respects—see what things were like at this battle for 'em. Get a different perspective, don' cha know. That Union jacket you have on has got to be mighty hot."

"Paying my respects. It's the least I can do, see what living in the heat musta been like."

"You from around here?"

"No—well in a way—granddad was from Dinwiddie."

"Yesterday, I said to you we would approach this battle in retrograde; I want to change that a bit. History is a living, breathing enterprise, not etched in stone. As we gather more information, more letters, more pictures and records, we refocus our efforts to get our interpretations exact, both qualitatively and quantitatively. Two primary accomplishments came about as the result of the civil war—freedom for the slaves and a solitary union—a republic, a nation governed as a democracy. Contemporary historians, and that includes military historians, are making significant efforts to include the role of the black soldier in the battles in which they participated. This has not been easy and not all historians agree on the impact of the African-American soldiers during the Civil War. Two of the most significant battles of the Civil War, the battle at Fort Pillow and the Battle of the Crater, were subject to review by the Congress of the United States. In both instances extraordinary effort was taken to ferret out the truth; the truth with relation to attitudes of the Confederate troops towards black soldiers and the attitudes of Union troops and their leadership toward black soldiers."

"On the Confederate side, General Patrick Cleburne repeatedly approached Jeff Davis on the efficacy of using black troops. Davis refused. On the Union side, General Benjamin Butler engaged African Americans as a pragmatic way to win the war. He was followed in this methodology by George H. Thomas at Nashville. The Congressional review of the Battle at Fort Pillow takes pains to interview and document the atrocities seen by Union militarists, black and white. Black, at that time called colored, soldiers were specifically interviewed in that document. To the best of my knowledge, no black soldier was interviewed and documented in the Congressional review document after the Battle of the Crater, though many survived. Even a Medal of Honor winner did not have his perceptions and opinions recorded in that document. A meta-comparison may give you an indication of the attitudes of the time, on both sides. I encourage you to read both documents and make your own decisions."

"Now the USCTs are listening and speculating. They are scrutineers one and all, and guess what? They are fully awake. Their pride is hurt because the job they trained for has been given to someone else—and mind you—they trained hard for that gig: zigzags, hurdles, running with footbridges, firing on the dead run, company movements, memorizing military objectives. Remember that most of them could not read. It's almost 8:00 am and do they have moxie? Oh yeah," said the female tour guide, answering her own question.

A voice, chiming like dropped keys and scratchy—*from yelling?*— sounded behind his ear. "I knew those boys, all good soldiers, but challenged in different ways. Weaver had a wonderful singing voice— couldn't read in daylight! Slavery kept him in its grasp. Could only read after sundown, in a corner closet, with a small lantern. Damn near suffocated trying to read that way. Porter over there almost got court-martialed 'cause he just could not salute and look an officer in the eye. Where he came from, you never, ever looked directly at Massa. *Always kept your eyes fixed on the ground, nigga!*. The colored chaplains kept those boys singing; confiscated moonshine, cards, dice—taught some reading too. That South Carolina and Georgia psyche was amazing;

Mississippi too. For some of them boys, zigzagging came real natural. They would zig over to one side of the street, or zag to the other if they saw a white officers coming. Great training for guerrilla warfare. Skill came in real handy in dat Crater." Jalen frowned in bewilderment fish-eying for the speaker.

Two brown-skinned mimes approach the group in Union uniforms and bow deeply before the crowd; they take their positions at the entrance and make staggered zips to Cemetery Hill, before planting a Union flag.

"When they reach Cemetery Hill, they are met with a galling fire," said the guide.

The mimes run back, retrieve the flag thus planted, rush back and urge forth, pantomime a rally of their beleaguered troops capturing prisoners along the way.

"So, we know from letters and eyewitness accounts—diaries and letters, of the atrocities that took place at the Crater: bayoneting of blacks by white Unionists seeking preferential treatment by captors, surrendering blacks and whites being unmercifully murdered, blacks and whites being stalled and slaughtered in the Crater. There were also reports of black Confederate teamsters firing into the melee. All that darkness has some redeeming light; through trial and error, Grant is gradually making his way to Appomattox."

"What were the conditions for the Medal of Honor winner—how did that happen?" said Jalen.

"Thank you for your question—the question is how did Decatur Dorsey, of the USCT 39th accomplish his feat of planting a flag at Cemetery Hill, retrieving it, capturing prisoners, and rallying his troops. My answer is simple and you may find another in your research; Dorsey was literate, he could read and write, he was speedy—as in fast runner—and a fast learner, and he had Siegfried at his back! When you have a trusted and respectful friend like that, anything is possible!"

"Okay my friends," said the tour guide leading the group to the tunnel entrance. "This is where the Union soldiers entered the Crater. Imagine that you see a large funnel cloud of white smoke—timbers, human and animal limbs flying through the air, clouds of debris and humidity circling above, horses rearing in the air. Bring with you that fetid smell you inhaled last night plus the yells and commands of division leaders. Remember that Ledlie was not with his troops—nor was Ferrero."

The mimes ran into the depths of the Crater, bewildered and crazed, trying to orient themselves as if they had no idea of what to do next.

"Now over yonder, see the rebel troops, looking aghast at the sight. At what has just happened to Elliott's salient—the point of attack at Fort Pegram—and the sight of their comrades and fort suddenly airborne. Remember that Burnside and Meade are both tied to the telegraph, *behind* the front lines. The colored troops—USCTs—have been ordered to be the *last* to attack the breach, even though they trained for three weeks to lead this enterprise. Instead of going around the perimeter of the Crater, the first three divisions of white Union troops penetrate a huge foxhole, twenty to thirty feet deep. That cràter will become a trap—a fish barrel. As the Confederates recover, they wheel canon to the hole and fire musketry into the Union position." Grayback mimes indicate the rebel rally."

Next, another pair of uniformed Union mimes led the second division— the men of Potter's division—into the Crater. The mimes stumble around as if in a fog, tap one another as if to ask for directions, and began to fire back at the recovering rebels starting to line the rim of the crater. Far behind them, three figures–posing as grave diggers with shovels thrown over their backs—strummed guitars and hummed quietly. To Jalen, one of them looks familiar. *He's too far away to be heard.*

"They are followed by yet another division. Remember that a division at this time was comprised of up to six thousand men. These are the men of Willcox's division; so you can imagine the chaos that was developing given the debris, the heat, the lack of clear leadership, and the smoke. As the morning progresses, white soldiers looking as smoky and sooty as the Africans some of them detested poured out of the Crater. Three divisions had gone in already; this became a major human traffic jam, with Confederates firing freely into the mess.

Someone voiced, "Where is Ferrero?" *They look defeated.*

"Ergo, our USCTs. They are the fourth division to pour into the Crater at around 8:00 o'clock in the morning. Bedlam and confusion greet their eyes as they witness the wounded streaming out of the breach and furious firing and hand-to-hand combat in the Crater. It is a spectacle with hell written all over it. What do they do? They execute as trained for the most part; up until about 10:30, when we arrive at a stalemate, with the Confederate troops of General Mahone stemming the advance of Union troops, short of Jerusalem Plank road. Burnside was later furious at the changes in attack order and Grant later acknowledged that the Crater *could* have been a success if the USCTs had been put in first."

Jalen reflected silently on the dilemma faced by the black soldiers. "God," he thought, "these men, a team of African-Americans called the United States Colored Troops, listened with ears stretched 360 degrees as they watched the wounded stream out of "Dat huge hole in the ground!" Bridge to freedom or hell? They'd sketched, planned, rehearsed, and exercised, and made tactical alterations to achieve mastery. They'd subjected those tactics to trial and error, revision, measurement, and memorization to become a team. As a snowfall of Minie balls pockmocked the rim of the dusty bowl forming their target, they assaulted the enemy in a battered bowl of bog-downed blue-coats."

"Before that moment, they'd been rendered fallow in a theater of the absurd," said the guide. She continued, "So we have a meta-bridge between two Congressional Boards of Review, to help us understand racial attitudes in context, to the step-by-step revelations of changes in the order of battle. What would have happened if the USCTs had been put in first? Would there have been the same result? Orr maybe a different one? That is a question to which we will never know the answer! Lastly, there is continued controversy about Confederate General Nathan Bedford Forrest. Consider that he and Frederick Douglass were both self-taught and self-educated geniuses; they learned how to teach themselves. Learning is the key ingredient to both personalities. George C. Marshall wrote about his classes at the Army Staff College. 'But I learned how to learn; my habits of thought were being trained.' So, perhaps one could say the *sculpting* of one's habits of thought is the key ingredient seized from the study of history. Folks, you have been a terrific audience. Many, many thanks for your attention. Now please stay for the musketry exhibition which will be right at the crest of Cemetery Hill."

XXIII

Jalen had found his car parked a good ways from Cemetery Hill. He'd spun the key, spent minutes trying to crank the ignition thinking, "Jeeze, I'm hungry—get on the road and grab a burger while I'm driving." He placed a call to Chelsea, "Hey baby. 'Bout to get on the road. Having a little trouble getting my car started. It's either the starter or the battery... hope to be there shortly. Should take me about three hours; don't wait up."

"Did you have a good time?"

"It was pretty interesting—the tour guide was just great—everybody did an excellent job."

He raised the reddish sunglasses up on his hairline noting the bone-white clouds against a muddy, darkening skyline. While under the hood to check the battery, he heard a faint hum of "Shu dubie dubie du."

"Hey fellas. How are you boys doing?"

"Oh fine Mr. Harkness, just fine. You having trouble with your whip?"

"Doesn't seem to want to start. Can I get a boost off you guys?" He kept his face emotionless, hoping they would miss his flash of recognition. *Shit, these are those damn gravediggers.*

"Oh yeah, we can do that."

As he lifted his gaze up from the battery, the double barrel of a shotgun growled at his eye-balls.

"Get in our wheels Harkness—I'll take the phone." The three men leered at him, anticipating motion.

"What about my car?"

"Don't worry about that; after all, it's just another whip," said Felder holding the piece while the other two wrenched his arms backwards, handcuffing him. "Loaf," said Felder, "pull his shades down so his spirits stays rosy." Loaf strong-armed him into the SUV, grabbed the shotgun from Felder, and sat behind him in the backseat. "Bo, light a cigar for me son—put some tea in it."

Bo lit the blunt, poured cheap gin into paper cups, and rolled himself a joint. "Da-da...d—shit, this don feel lak no highway—m-mo-moe lak a b-b-bone-plank road, bumpy-as-shit."

The Varina-Enon Bridge sparkled through the purplish haze inside the passenger compartment like over-sized daggers, lodged in the bridge from underneath. Jalen fought to breathe oxygen where none was to be had. The combination of sunglasses, haze and contact high comingled, corrupting his senses. "Where are we going guys, where are you taking me?" The handcuffs burned his wrists, but he stayed relaxed in the passenger seat, the gun barrel nuzzled against his back. Bo pig-eyed the complaining passenger shining a gold grin.

***

In the kingdom of her consciousness, the woman juried the juncture of mind and heart, spirit and soul. She sought to rein in the psychic chaos of American apartheid; soothe the anguished souls of the depressed, the frustrated, the poor, the disheartened, the black. She had intimate knowledge of the psychological terrain, the lingering superstitions of slavery. She had hers too. For her, there were two balms, two polarities—religious fervor or psychic dissolution. Between those polarities, between those opposites, on occasion stood education–if appetite flourished beyond tradition. There was a time when, for many coloreds—called African-Americans or blacks now—when church was the only place, outside of home, where they were appreciated for merely being able to breathe—and church celebrated that breath in song. She had grown to specialize in the mystical and occult. Even down the stepped passageway, the flicker of the "Readings" sign outlined her silhouette; her scans around the room captured the implements of her trade; a crystal ball, a prisoner's pillory and post; a projector that blossomed forth holograms in three dimensions. As she slowed to take deep, long breaths, the phone rang.

"We got him."

"Good bring him to me; keep him blindfolded. No fist-a-cuffs! Call me as you approach D.C. We'll put him in the séance parlor."

"Yes'm."

"Were they successful?" asked the other voice. "Did they get him?"

"Signed, sealed—practically delivered," said the voice on the other end, hearing the question.

"Oh goodie—it's par-ty time," said the second woman." She housed a volume of jealousy and hate well known to those who excel in the workplace; she had also known love, but that was long, long ago, in another time and place, where Primus Chambliss had her back—her butt, mind—her pussy, too. But everything, anything she had was not enough. Now unfavored professionally, she courted hate unfettered with a primal venom one hundred percent pure. It is a state of mind known well to those who have experienced the volcanic hatred of one compelled to animus, who hates out of compulsion.

"Do you understand what you are to do—understand your role?"

"Hell yeah." They shared tokes of a blunt, sniffed a bit of coke and proceeded to dress for the occasion.

The first woman slipped into black tights and put masks and riding crops on the large oval table. *Stupid bitch. All you think about is 'oh yeah.' I got a big surprise for you and your fat ass.* "Okay well keep those questions close at hand. You are Decatur Dorsey, you read the script first, do you understand?"

The second woman dressed too—hers was a long, black Friar Tuck's robe, with the sleeves rolled up.
"Yeah, sure," she answered.

"We'll put him in the séance parlor at the beginning—by himself; let him get a real good dose of Dorsey; then he gets to go on trial with your questions. I've got the mannequin in place. Then you can ask about his role in that 'no pay' suspension you got—make him think twice about playing the *esteemed* one, the pride of Claremont. Decatur Dosey *first.* Use the voice whiteout on the microphone and stay in the anteroom until I give you the word."

***

"You'll see soon enough."

By the time they reached the exit for Fredericksburg, the sign seemed to dance inverted against its green background. At the Sousa Bridge, he peered through the cabin's haze, locked his eyes on a bright, tan merry-go-round, checkered by the passing of gaslights standing on tall bones. He fought to focus sight. At the footsteps of the Watergate, the red tunics of the Marine Band spun counterclockwise to the tune of "John Brown's Body." Black soldiers in mime-face marched across the bridge, southward, singing, bow-bent. The trills of clarinets, blare of trumpets, and flash of cymbals strobed Bo's gold teeth as he slipped a blindfold under Jalen's rosy sunglasses soon after they crossed the bridge.

"Okay, now when you get out, listen well. We'll tell you when steps are in front of you—here is one step." A woman's voice, muffled in undertones, had met them as they stepped down a path, onto a sidewalk, up concrete stairs: *long fingernails.*

"There is a door-sill here, step over it, we are almost done—atta boy" More darkness except for occasional shards of light. He grazed the door jam—"Ouch." Now beyond the door stood more darkness. Then an entryway of some sort, carpet, and down stairs, carpeted at first, now wooden.

"Careful on the stairs—turn right—now we are heading down several steps; be careful. *Dank smell, cigarette smoke—maybe a blunt—weird buzzing sound—others present?* Through the blindfold, he could notice a focused brightness and then it died; *a flashlight?* After roping him tightly to the chair, Bo removed his blindfold, cuffed his right arm to the footrest of a high back chair.

"Now leave us. Leave him in the parlor, double check that knot, give me the keys for those cuffs. Good job boys."

Footsteps faded, retreating to another room—*an anteroom?* Bound, re-cuffed, and free of blindfold, he sat alone peering into a darkness pierced by sputtering and flutters of fluorescent light; *from somewhere else, another room perhaps above—above the steps they had descended.*

"Mr. Harkness, welcome to our party," came a computerized, micro-phoned voice, distorted in such a way that it was not possible to discern gender. Thank you so much for coming and for being such a good sport about the conditions of your—uh—presence. You have been such a busy fella, rummaging here and there, all over the east coast—a real learning machine. I understand you have a great interest in Decatur Dorsey. We wanted you to have the chance to meet him personally; do you care for a glass of wine? Whiskey?"

"No—I'm good."

"Greetings, Jalen," said a stentorian voice. "Thank you for your interest in my efforts at the Crater."

The image initially seemed a photograph, one of a black Civil War soldier, though he had been unable to find one of Dorsey in his own research. Holographic and translucent, it hovered, flamed and then, morphed animate, three dimensional.

"Yes, that was some enterprise there at the Crater. I'd heard Douglass speak in Baltimore and was inspired by his words. Luckily, as you can tell by my pension documents, I could read and write. That was truly an asset at the time—or at any time—as you well know. My master gave me permission to join the Union effort, under certain conditions. Of course, I would be free if the Union won—but, should the Union lose—then I would return to my master's plantation under the same conditions as before. That was the agreement between two honorable men. To be honest with you, one of my major concerns right before going into that Crater was if my suspenders would hold up. Artillery shells and minie balls screaming all around. Several of us had dysentery right before the explosion—I guess some of the horses did too. They dropped some mighty cowpies when that powder went off; the smells were horrible. By the way, those rifled artillery shells bear a striking similarity to those galvanized trash cans you have down there; suppose you can end up either with artillery in you or you in the artillery—either way, death brought her sharpest scythe that night. The rifling made the shells more accurate—stabilized the spin."

"'Hitch your britches laddies.' That was the call of the moment. Right before, 'charge!' Charge and make sure your gun is loaded—course, me carrying colors, I had me a pistol. *Siegfried* was the main one who worked with us. I consider him a friend to this day...ahem. We did sprints daily, drills in Napoleon type volleys, firing at will—lots of drill on loading fast and faster, firing by rank and by file—some of the fellas 'round me talkin' 'bout remember Fort Pillow!' *For some, the more rebs dey shot, the more halos dey gits in heaven.* Had some turncoats too. Pissed Fleetwood off sumthin' terrible. They made me a leader 'cause I could read and run pretty fast. Most a those poor boys couldn't read a lick—from what I hear about ch'all, that still be the case. Boys back then would hide it out of shame; looks to me like as fast as they finds out a flock of black boys are around, they pulls all the reading teacher outta those schools you got down there. That's the advantage you got when you're a ghost. You gets to fly anywhere—Detroit, D.C., Memphis, N'awleans—all over. Anyways, you could tell that old Ferrero was a chicken-shit; kept away from the men, called 'em niggers real regular. Never did learn their names, and couldn't outrun a mule.

"'They ain't been trained, they run too slow, ain't nary footbridge, whars de ladders? Been aiming for dis chance four mons'.". The niggers said that when the white units went in; does that word offend you? Those phrases came to me—mellifluous, I *love* that word mellifluous, in a musical flurry, just like the colors of the men who voiced them; tan, purplish black, mahogany, walnut brown—beige highlighted with magenta." The apparition spun grandly, levitated and continued,

"I'd reinforced the buttons on my suspenders. I could stand a lot of things—*but I hate for my pants to slide down when I'm runnin'. That damn slap on the back of my neck squished something;*I took away my hand

and examined a streak of blood—*a dead mosquito—wonder whose...if it was Yankee or Johnnie.* Took out my handkerchief and wiped away both blood and insect, then I re-hitched my suspenders, tightened my shoestrings, clutched the colors, the USCT flag."

"Told you all that prep shit was fake. We bought it too, right down to the damn explosion! Grandberry, a dark-skinned kid in my unit said that. Said this too , 'The white man is *never* to be trusted.' It was talk I'd heard before. Look at this description," said Dorsey. He sat cross-legged on the table and read.

"The explosion, mammoth in sound, terrified the horses, shocked quietude, ripped and rippled in underground belches. On the heels of the sharp thunderclap, deafening aftershocks cannonaded stereophonically, followed by a tornadic whoosh of white smoke. Violent tongues of rapacious fire licked trees, limestones, ramparts, butternuts, and grilled the smoke itself. Billows of dark smoke waltzed above the open sore as flashes of airborne body parts rode astride moonbeams and reclined on smoky clouds overlooking a gnash in the earth—perceived by attackers as a foxhole. Flames inhaled oxygen and seared devilish graffiti on the early morning sky," said the ghost smiling, "or this one,"

"'Man and mule cursed foul oaths. Swaths of yellow, red, orange, groaned in gulps, screams, and farts, while heat hammered the ground underfoot. Black plumes danced up ladders of smoke; sound warred with vision as the vortex separated spirit from bone. Emancipated, the man-made inferno vulcanized tree-branches, roasted and toasted unsuspecting graycoat sentries in a hellish burlesque. My, my—how some historians capture truth; oh to be black and *scribe free* in Virginia territory."

"I heard one of my boys scream, 'Old man Pleasants brought hell right to the earth. I found this pistol, a six-shooter; you being the color-bearer, you shore as hell gon' need it. Wafts of latrine stench leeched to sulfur, sewer and garbage smells, further poisoning the air. The devil hisself is present and accounted for." The apparition seemed more frenzied, rose to full height and said,

"Saw y'all visited old Ebenezer Creek too—now *there* was a mess," he said: "Those textbooks the kids read makes the number of drowned slaves smaller every year. Think about it. Sherman marched from Atlanta to Savannah, and only three hundred drowned at 'Nezer Creek. Flat out stupidity. You want to understand the attitude of the time, put those congressional reviews side by side—read 'em. Blacks interviewed at Pillow, not at the Crater. Black soldiers there, I was there, but their voices—*had no scribe!* Our ghosts lurk yet, *but you got to read to find 'em.* You may see me as a ghost now, but I was a ghost *then!* Our practices had become more perfect; gold watches played their part with each beginning producing a more efficient end.

'Faster Dorsey!' We ran: with ladders, with foot bridges, with hatchets and bayonets. We gained in stamina, executing as a unit, changing methods focusing on guerrilla warfare. *We sang, chanted and echoed in choruses*—low, run low to the ground, in squads of four, the best shooters crossing directions, the best runners zigzagging with the flag, all cross-training for a range of possibilities. We became a team. Now, I'll not tarry much longer other than to say much obliged for your interest. The boys of the 39th appreciate and thank you for your remembrances."

Another whitewashed voice, different in pace and tone, spoke.

"Okay Harkness. We have arranged for you to witness another bit of slave history. It is, I admit, a crude replica compared to the formal entertainment you have witnessed over the weekend; however, this demonstration is intended for you—and you alone. With that in mind, I present to you chapter one of 'Skip the Whip,'a mini-drama in two parts—in reality two chapters. The first chapter features our mannequin—let's call her Lady Harkness, in salute of your lovely wife

Chelsea. Now Chelsea has been a bad girl lately and she refuses to answer the questions we put to her—or answers them incorrectly. Kind of like one of your exams, but here the wrong answer gets you a lashing or two—call it *retro discipline, Gothic discipline, slave discipline.* While you're watchin' our wee demonstration, visualize—*feel*—yourself as that mannequin, 'cause you gon' have your turn."

Draped in a black ski mask and a monkish, hooded black robe, the figure snatched a black riding crop and strolled to the place where an early American wooden prisoner's stock—some call it a pillory—stood on its post. Clasped in its' holes was a male mannequin of indistinct features, that stood at a height of about six feet. The figure rared back and swung the crop against the back of the mannequin, causing it to buckle and jack-knife violently. *Swung as if delivered by—a woman?*

"Well done," said Jalen, "Now exactly what is my role in all of this? I have never whipped a student or anyone else taking one of my exams." Instinctively, he tested the strength of the cuff; he felt his heart race slightly faster, felt blood race faster through his veins, nodded against his fists to wipe sweat from his forehead.

"We call this 'Skip the Whip.' Whip-skip—I like that! Now Harkness, I know you are used to being in charge, being in control. But those who know you—know of that intellectual crap, Civil War history, scientific methods, creative problem-solving crap that you are teaching these kids, we think *you* need a lesson in being trained—being malleable— *manageable.* That's it, manageable. Black folk stood steady, stood straight up under the whip and the collar; some say it did 'em good, cleansed them of provocateurs. *Remember, the more halos dey gits in heaven.* They were trained *to obey!*"

"Now, me and Decatur Dorsey has got some questions—*after-lecture*— post-lecture, questions for you, since you likes to give tests and all. Your tutor there's gone stand behind that mannequin—of course it can't jump, hog-tied like that to a yoke—but you can Jalen—yes indeed, *you can*. Now, I'm gonna ask you some questions and friend there is going to show you how the game plays out for answers that are, using collegiate terminology, incorrect. Hope you don't mind. Stand up! Oh, I forgot, you're tied to that seat. Tutor—unbind, unharness Mr. Harkness—oh my ha-ha, Harkness unharnessed, what will we come up with next. He's got to be able to practice his jumpin'."

He felt the ropes and tape bindings gradually unravel; *now is the time to run.*

"Oh and by the way, those three gentlemen are right outside that door you just glanced at."

"Damn," he thought.

XXIV

"Can't sleep, shoot. I like having my guy around. Maybe I'm too used to climbing up his back when he's tucked in, nice and warm. Wonder if he got the car started. I'll call him."

Chelsea had dialed the number three times before realizing that she would not get a human voice. All she got was that tune by Drumma Boy, "Where I Come From." Unsatisfied with that result, she went back to bed, closed her eyes and sought sleep—but sleep escaped her, even after she tried several attempts at favored positions; she fluffed her pillows, practiced taking deep breaths, lay at lengths on her back: *nada.* Chelsea got up, grabbed the card they had left in her studio from Royce. She studied the card, fisted the phone, and dialed the numbers.

"Hallo."

"Royce—look I'm sorry to call you at this hour, but I'm worried."

"Worried? I'm sorry, who am I talking to?"

"Oh, oh. Royce this is Chelsea Harkness."

"Oh hey Chelsea. Great seeing you guys the other night. Didn't catch your voice right away. You say you are worried, worried about what?"

"Look—Jalen went down to Petersburg for a re-enactment of the Crater...the Battle of the Crater, this weekend. He called earlier, said he was headed home, but also said he was having some car trouble—starter or battery trouble. I just called him—three times—to check on him. Didn't get an answer. I wonder if there is anyway for you to trace— check on him. I just have a bad feeling about this; *please say you have a way to help me contact him.* Anyway, can you help me? Can you do something to help me find him? Maybe I'm overreacting, but I think something has happened to him. He always stays in good touch with me."

"Yeah, I know Jalen—he's not one to ignore ya, or any friend, when they try to reach him: *dependable*. Okay. I've got some favors I can call in. This is my home phone—give me your number and I'll call you back in a few. I'm sure we'll find out what's going on. By the way, is this a smartphone he uses?"

"Oh yes. He loves that thing—a little less than me of course. He said he might use it to find his way to the battlefield, said he hadn't been there before."

"Good. I think I have the number, but just in case, give it to me."

Chelsea recited Jalen's number for his smart-phone. "Oh thank you Royce. Thank you so much."

"No problem. I'll be in touch."

Royce thought for a minute or two, donned his transvestite outfit, grabbed his 357 magnum, and called his contact at his home precinct. He also called one of his buddies at the FBI office in downtown D.C.

"Frank—Look I have a buddy, an old high school chum, who went down to a Civil War reenactment down in Petersburg this weekend.

172

His wife just called me thinking that he may have met with some sort of misfortune. She has tried to call him several times. I tried it too—getting a recorded message. Can you do me a favor and see if you can track, put a trace on his GPS system? I have the number for his cell phone."

"No problem Royce—I'll talk to the troopers down in Virginia too. This your number?"

"Yep. I've got a hunch I'm going to follow. Saw some of those guys–those gravedigger fellas, 'Bottom's Up,' eye-ballin' us at Turk's the other night—the ones that hang out at the Circle sometimes, Ebenezer Hill too. Don't know for sure if they are involved in this. I know Turk is fairly conservative...maybe a Confederate sympathizer—know that he may have been going down there. Anyway, I've talked too long. See if you can find out anything." He gave Frank Lombardi the number he'd written down adding, "and thanks!"

Royce hopped in his squad car; the force had him take the car home as a means of policing high crime areas, though his street was fairly safe. He put on his official badge, cranked the engine, cruised up towards Ebenezer Hill, but at a nominal speed, no flashing lights. Halfway there, his phone rang.

"Royce?"

"Yo—talk to me."

"Just got a callback from the trooper's office down near Petersburg. They found Harkness' car not far from that re-enactment they had down there. Hood was still up. Said it didn't look like any foul play was involved—looked like he may have had some car trouble of some sort. But get this—the signal for his smart-phone is coming from a D.C. location."

"Copy."

"Where are you now? You heading up to 'Nezer Hill?'"

"Halfway there."

"I got backup headed up there. Called your precinct—you need support from us?"

"Better safe than sorry, if you got folks to spare."

"You got it—running cost is dinner. Be safe."

***

Jalen studied his options; *you think long, you think wrong*. He heard mangled, filtered words coming through the microphone, but it was on his periphery. *You better think right this night lil' bro*. The round table was sturdy; much too heavy and thick to move, too weighty to heft in seconds. *But the crystal ball—that could be hefted easily*. "I would like to take that glass of water now—maybe two, one of water and one of that whiskey you mentioned. Jack Daniels if you got it."

Gold gleamed past Bo's smirk; the abductor growled from the hallway, saying, "I'll g-g-get it."

Jalen espied the electric chord leading to the table and listened...*one, two, three, four ,five, six, seven....Nine steps?*

He caught movement in the sidebar of his sunglasses, careful not to give away direction by turning his head.

"Now think carefully—the catch is, you have got a real good chance of missin' that lickin' when you hear the whip sing in the air. If—you *jump* in time. So this is gonna be..."

"...a lesson in listening," offered Jalen, "with serious consequences if I give the wrong answer. I might skip the whippin' if I jump in time, even if my answer is wrong. Gimme a sample question." He smiled hearing the Marine Band whirl through the Battle Hymn, seeing the hologram dim, listening for footfalls, flexing a creak in the chair.

"Ahhhh...that famous curiosity. Let's see, you have criticized black clergy in D.C., saying that they should have literacy labs, computer banks for tutoring kids and adults right in the churches, supporting literacy—do you think your charges have merit?"

"Many kids have parents, grandparents, aunts, uncles who read poorly if at all. It's an inter-generational cycle of illiteracy. Reading the bible is fine, but there are three-hundred sixty degrees of global culture out there to be read about. Some individuals control their flock with either mysticism or the Bible...*halos in heaven.* Of course my charges have merit."

"Wrong!!!"

He watched as the inanimate mannequin absorbed a furious flurry of lashes. The object buckled and danced as Bo brought water and whiskey in two separate glasses. *Damn. Could be a very long night if I live through it.* The glasses stood on the table. Bo turned the corner; *one, two..... ten steps.* Jalen's ears flashed; he was sure he heard the "ding-dong" of a doorbell. *Chaos—create chaos.*

"Okay," he thought. *I've got seconds to lob the crystal ball, toss water and whiskey at electrical outlets; no, better to cannonball that crystal ball, bomb the anteroom, crash the chair, yank that mannequin, hammer whatever comes my way and trip whoever comes down those steps. Think long, think wrong…better think right tonight. Kick the table. That round table—upend it with your thighs, make it roll. Think long, think wrong.*

NOW! In a series of swift movements, he leapt skyward, brought his weight down on the chair. It broke, freed his arms, allowed him use of a spindle as a nightstick. *Spindle in your teeth.* Jalen cradled the crystal ball and flung it back over his head; *CRASH*; He quick-fisted both glasses, tossing them towards electrical outlets; *SIZZLE, ZAPS, BLACKOUT.* His plunge into a squat voided the zing of a crop swung in his direction.

"ASSHOLE," rung in his ears as he hefted the table up with his thighs. It lumbered and rolled towards the doorway. "UGHhhhgh," strafed the room in a long, high-pitched scream as a luminous skeleton streaked fancifully in its' wake, a deflated balloon.

"Spin move, spin move, stay close to the ground—NOW!" A voice whispered, "Fist the chair spindle, yank the mannequin."

Jalen yanked the mannequin—*the strawman*—from its yoke (unfortunately the yank tore the hands from plastic sockets). He spun on his heels, whirling it across the steps to trip runners downwards, forcing their fall to the lower level and he swung the spindle at the sparkle springing his way; *contact!*

"Owwww…ff-f-fu-fuckin' idiot…godjjammit!"

Another swing silenced everything but distant clatter, electrical sizzles, upper-level gunshots. A blizzard of stuttered gunshots diced seconds. A cratered eruption—pock-marked, dusty and smoke-laden, yawned as a morning haze and floated over dappled blazes. The eruption lit monstrous shadows. He heard angry yells, stumbled over dead bodies, saw furious fighting and sparkled flashes of bayonets. *Hands clammy;*

was that a bugle? He leapt over bushy ground fire, and past a foggy, smoky hash of embers.

"Run low, watch the steps," the Voice whispered.

Someone had run down the steps, slipped, tripped on the prone mannequin, fallen and lost his ..."

"Damn, Motherf...!"

"Bang...bang, bang..." more shots roared from up the stairs. The man who had fallen limped upright, took a furious swing at Jalen. The huge fist sped towards him, knuckles pointed at his nose. He froze for a split second, hypnotized by its movement. He ducked, dipped, then spun again; *still near wake!* He jumped, swung, rippled his elbows, kicked, thought he heard his name. His spindle-swings strobed against the beam of a flashlight—*coming from upstairs?*

"Aaai—eeeee!" A sharp scream ripped the air. He half-smelled a pungent odor, back-stepped seeing flares of electric sizzles. Jalen rolled into a spin-move, cuff-yanked the pillory-post down on the man's lower body. A shard of battery powered flashlight criss-crossed the passageway then a flash of shadows dappled against light; *bang—from where?*

"Jalen, Jalen—you down there?"

In the last quarter of that split second, he ducked and pushed, hoping his next punch would find the flesh indicated by that last mental snapshot; *nothing, missed!* He followed-up, kicked and shouldered the flash of a man's back, smashing it face-first into concrete, metal rattled on the floor.

"Yeah!"

"Mommy, mommy! I heard gunshots. What's happening? What's happening? That man! That's the same man that—mommy that's Mr. Harkness!!"

Another abductor, shot at the door entrance by Royce, left a trail of blood as he fled. A short distance from the door, you could hear the vehicle, the one they had ridden in, screeching and burning rubber towards a day-long getaway. Ms. Dennison, half-robed and electrocuted, lay trapped between wiring and pools of water, horribly disfigured. Her hair still crackled from electric surges; the body smelt of burning flesh; *cratered!*

XXV

"I think we make a pretty good team," said Chelsea, "especially after all that chaos. Your buddy Royce really came through for us—we should have him over for a *real* dinner—one we make all together. "

"That's a good idea—I'll check in with him, see what he's got up. That was a real close call—darn it. What did I ever do to Dennison? We rarely talked; I hardly knew the chick. And her and Queen Esther as a team— oh boy. Well you are the captain of this team—thank goodness; great intuition. Guys get to develop those 'got-your-back' skills, both on the sandlot and on supervised teams. Royce and I had those skills between us from jump street—right from the beginning. Chelsea, you're a great blessing for my back, front too—ahem."

"You know, now that you mention it, that may be a good place to start with Damisi and Tofu—have them be a team somehow." She hummed, massaged his shoulders and elbows as she spoke, kneading the stiff muscles with strong fingertips. "I enjoyed talking to them in your class and I bet they will do a outstanding report. "

"You think so?" he said, bringing his eyes to meet hers, "Did you play on a team, play team sports?'

"I was on teams—sort of. The girls on my block imitated the boys sometimes, even played with the boys, when we were very young. We got dusty and mud-caked playing on that softball field right across from the house. Why, I betcha we got every bit as smoky as those soldiers down at the Crater."

"Funny you mentioned that. A coupla guys down at the Crater—black fellas—were crackin' up over hearin' the term, 'smoked yankees'; they'd never heard the term before."

"Really, what's so funny about that?"

"That's what our Anglo brethren in the south called black soldiers— 'smoked yankees.'"

"Ha-ha, that is kinda funny—depending on the source, you understand. Have you spoken with Chambliss yet? I'm sure he's chomping at the bit to get your take on all these events."

"Yeppy. He wants me in on a pow-wow he's arranged with Solomon; it's especially important since the court has awarded him temporary custody of Tofu. Be interesting to see how he steps up to the plate, him being white and all. Real interesting."

"Wonder how he and Queen Esther got together?"

"Trapped by the "P" word, probably—the downfall of many a brave Yankee or rebel for that matter."

"You guys are all the same—spellbound by that "P" thang you be mentionin'," she retorted, grazing him gently with her left hip. "I told them I would meet with them if they cleared it with you."

"What did they say to that?"

"All for it. What do *you* say?"

"You have my thankful blessings. Did I hear you say something about play?"

They hung out most of the day Monday. Chambliss had given him the day off after learning about the weekend's events. On Tuesday, he asked his class, "How are you coming along with those reports?" The question prompted a ton of questions; can we use music—musical instruments? Can we sing in rap poetry? Can we use the projector; how about photos, can we use those? Do we have to turn in a typed paper? Can we make a movie instead? And last but not least, "Were you in a big fight?"

Earlier, he had remembered that he had on the same jacket that he'd worn to the Lincoln Memorial; feeling the presence of the dark red sunglasses in the inside pocket jarred him at first. Stopping as he passed the teacher's lounge, he had soaped the glasses, rinsed, and washed them. *But weren't they in the blue Union jacket?* They covered several bruises; *looked good.*

"Okay–how about this. You can do all of those questions including a typed report from each individual participant; however, you should collaborate—work as a team. In fact, you might find it fun to do your reports in a group or as part of a group—your choice."

Damisi raised her hand, "Tofu and me—we want to work in a group."

"Well lets do this. We'll have four teams and three symbols. The symbols are a blue ribbon, an iron chain, and a set of ears. Let's choose groups right now. Tofu and Damisi in this corner on Lincoln, Corliss over in that corner on General Thomas, Spence over here on Douglass, and Marsha there on Ebenezer Creek and Harpers Ferry. Vote with your feet; just gather around the topic that you want to deliver in a group report."

"Now in the final minutes, you can talk in your groups and do some group work. I'll need a typed paper from each individual though. I've got to run by the office. Do you need a sergeant-at-arms?"

A flock of "nos" pushed him out the door.

"General Harkness, comment sa va?" quipped principal Chambliss.

"Bien, et vous?" said Jalen in retort. "Much better now that nightmare of a weekend is over. Thanks for letting me take Monday off. I appreciate that. Except for the phone ringing off the hook, I got to take a long hot bath and spend some time lounging with team captain Chelsea Harkness."

"She okay?"

"Oh yeah. If she hadn't acted on those intuitive vibes she gets, I'd have been in deep doo-doo."

"Well come on in the office. I've set things up in tandem. First you and I should talk, go over the lay of the land before Solomon Turk gets here—been in his place a few times, always had a good time. I think he is actually part Scot and French. But who knows? I never really asked him where the Turk comes from. Anyway, the papers are trying to print whatever they can ferret out on that mess this weekend—damned Dennison really got herself jammed up with drugs floating around, drinking. God only knows what the coroner will find. I knew she had issues but, jeez—the woman was a mess. I really apologize to you on that one Jalen. I should have come clean on her esteem issues with you; we had what some would call a torrid affair when I first started teaching. I should have clued you in on that. Turned out to be a huge mistake—almost broke up my marriage. I never realized that she was flipped in such a state—her and Queen Esther—golly. I knew she was a refugee from the classroom, but not to the extent that it amounted to…and in guidance to boot. Well, she's gone now, poor devil.

The mother, Queen Esther has been arraigned, along with those gravediggers. The negative publicity worries me; another gift I don't need. Anyway, you're fine and we have Chelsea to thank—and Royce of course. You're lucky to have a friend like that. Oh, I think I hear Mr. Turk coming in; let's get him in here."

"Thank you for being frank Primus, I appreciate that too."

Through oblique angles of sunlight streaming into the office, Jalen considered regiments of suspended, golden dust; *days getting shorter*. Turk was in a subdued mood as he took a seat in the office. The shadows of the venetian blinds seemed to emphasize the lines drawn in his face—he seemed to have aged since the dinner when they had first met. Vertical lines in his face junctured with the shadowed, horizontal lines of the blinds, checker-boarding his face.

"Hi Harkness. I want to apologize for the actions of those grave-digging cohorts of mine; apparently, they were in cahoots with Esther— something I wasn't aware of. Hope your are coming off all this with no ill-feelings against me, and especially against Tofu. I really had no idea; fact is I almost made the reenactment—had some business things that caught me up at the last minute. She is really enjoying your class; I see a difference. And she was thrilled to meet your wife, Chelsea."

"Oh no—for me, that kind of thing takes way too much energy. And remember, it's Jalen. But say, I understand that the barn-house and even the cemetery have been in your family—or associated with your family for a long time. Rumor has it that there are both blacks and white buried there, dating back to the Civil war. Is that true?"

"As far as I know; those grave digger fellas were down there—or at least according to what they told me—looking for evidence of exactly that question. Told me their mission was exploratory. Looking for artifacts—bullets, belt buckles, cooking utensils. Said that some local archaeologists mentioned that a free slave community existed on that hill. Damned liars. I could wring their necks for that lie. Anyway, there is a myth that surrounds Ebenezer Hill, at least in family folklore—suggests that several black and white soldiers fought close to that Hill and the cemetery was employed as a communal grave—soldiers all mixed up. I can't vouch for its truthfulness."

"I see—just wondering."

"Look Harkness, I know very little about black history—just, for me, it was never a priority. Now we've got that African-American Civil War Memorial here in D.C. Even with the little I know, it does seem important to me that a person knows something of the battles, both civil and military, the black race has fought. Not just to be Americans but even beyond that—to be citizens of the world. Aware and knowledgeable about all cultures and civilizations. Knowledge is a human birthright; that is the whole point of engagement with nature and the meaning of living. I, myself, strive to become more universal, more aware of what it means to be continental. I almost feel like a fool bearing my soul like this."

"Well to be honest, Mr. Turk," said Chambliss, "I'm happy you understand what Mr. Harkness—Jalen—is trying to do, trying to accomplish with these youngsters. Many of these kids hate themselves—have internalized the rejection and abhorrence that the majority culture seems to hold for them. In many places, in places that only look at Tofu from the outside in, they will perceive her as being black—they couldn't give a whit if she had mixed parentage. Now we do have a gang problem that we are trying to throttle. Control. Jalen's approach—which I support—emphasizes the worth and dignity of each one of his students. And that

184

computer bank in his classroom is designed to support better, more skillful reading on their parts. That's what his effort with the tour was designed to enhance; self-esteem. As they become more independent in their thinking, our hope is that they will reject the simplistic thinking and autocratic procedures and values of gangs. Recent studies suggest that parental engagement is key to academic performance on the part of students. That is the theory," said Chambliss.

"Well, she read to me the other day—had these marshmallows in her mouth—and I still understood most of the words. She is with me until we find out more about what will happen with her mother."

"Thank you Chelsea," Jalen thought. He said, "I want to do everything I can to prevent a psychological death on the part of these youngsters. That was the aim of slavery and Jim Crow—to create a psychological death. Physical death is different and some slaves chose that. If we can get them to think comparatively and globally—not regurgitate, merely program and indoctrinate—then we have a chance of producing Americans—blue, green, black or yellow—who are healthy and continental citizens of the world. I never got to know your former wife. Don't know much about séances, reincarnation, getting in touch with ancestors—but I am committed to helping my students think. And I hope I have your support in that enterprise with Tofu. My objective is to create magnificent learners, regardless of color—or the shades of those colors."

"I think what Jalen is saying is that we have a legal responsibility to educate each and every student. We all have made mistakes, even teachers—and perhaps their unions. Jalen has tackled the ministers, but no teacher's union has sponsored reading improvement websites, not colleges and universities, nor major business enterprises. Our society has not committed to enabling the fullest development of all its citizens. We need your help in trying to change that; certainly we will not tolerate gangs or bullies. The police, ministers, psychologists, and webmasters are coordinating with us to contain bullying."

"Well I have to say that I have not been intimately involved with her academics, but I plan to do better. Is she in a gang now?"

"We don't think so, but she is being recruited. That business in the cafeteria was an initiation rite. It might be a good idea fo you to bring and pick her up at school for a week or two—'til things get sorted out."

"Okay. Well Jalen–Mr. Chambliss, I feel better after this talk. I will stay in close touch."

"Thank you Mr. Turk—we will do the same."

XXVI

"Okay my little scrutineer friends—today is the big day. We'll try to get to everybody today, but if necessary, we finish up tomorrow. Let's travel backwards in time for a few seconds. Just recently you have read and seen on television, numerous references to the 1963 'March on Washington,' which secured political power for blacks with legislation solidifying the right to vote. Prior to this was the Brown versus the Board of Education, which addressed separation of the races in education. The verdict was designed to secure quality education for all young Americans, regardless of race. Before that, came the integration of the armed services which was preceded by the debates of Booker T. Washington and W.E.B. Du Bois, with Du Bois advocating full access to the fruits of humanity in all cultural endeavors and Washington advocating separation of the races, and industrial education for blacks. Both men created institutions— Hampton University, the NAACP—which support and provide citizenship scaffolding for blacks to this day. Remember, at the time of the Civil War, blacks were not allowed to legally testify against whites in courts of law; that may be a factor in the racial differences of testimony between Fort Pillow and the Crater."

"Now, all this work in truth supports the creative gifts of every American, but as you have seen from our tour, all this has occurred from efforts to enable the development of each individual's human growth and development. Carl Jung—whom we won't examine in this class, says— 'The refusal of a higher development or higher consciousness is one of the most destructive things there is. Among other things, it makes people automatically pull back everyone else who tries to develop their creative gift—if you don't try to develop your creative gift, that energy turns to poison.' Your one sentence responses to Chelsea suggest not throwing your flowers or yourselves away. This school exists to enable your development into that state of higher creativity. So let's roll with your presentations; as you finish, put your papers on my desk."

A circus atmosphere permeated the room; students sporting masks, blue in various states of being, ears in a multiplicity of shapes, and an assortment of iron chains. Spence approached the front of the classroom first, accompanied by his entourage, each young man dressed to the nines in suit and tie. They huddled as if members of a football team, momentarily quiet and broke into a spellbinding growl.

"We are here today to speak of the work and efforts of the magnificent Frederick Douglass." The members of his team formed a semi-circle around him, echoing the words in chorus, "Frederick Douglass."

"I want to thank you for taking the time to visit with me at my estate recently, to see my library, listen to the music of my grandson, and see the Growlery. There were many times when I had to just go back out there and let off steam as the war for the preservation of the Union approached. We abolitionists..."

The group behind him echoed the word "abolitionists," on cue.

"...felt that the black man, so recently freed from his chains, should lend his great energy to the effort to secure his freedom. In gatherings both in this great Union and on the continent, many of our friends in this cause for humanity, welcomed and joined me in the effort to banish slavery from the face of the earth. They were tireless and fearless in those dark times, supplying money, food, and intellect on behalf of those who had endured the ravages and whip of the slave-master. We had to develop skillful written narratives, newspapers, pamphlets and posters to covey both our experiences and hopes, yearnings and fears."

A tenor voice continued, "And we had to constantly think of those we had left behind, those who were still in bondage, and develop creative strategies for helping them to secure their freedom. These chains remind me still of the bondage we endured, the whip, the cries, the songs we sang to lesson the pain of our experience and the prayers we sent upward to garnish the north star. But I also formed a chain of trust with the great President Lincoln, which cemented our friendship and the trust necessary to accomplish great effort. The blue," and the group unfurled the Civil War flag of the Union, "signifies both the joys and sorrows of the black soldier, teamsters, cooks, washerwomen, scouts, spies, and laborers who were devoted to the cause of freedom. The chains that bound us prior to the war..." and the group echoed, "prior to the war, were forever broken." Then they growled individually, leaning backwards and forwards as a passing wave. Spence then picked up the chain, stepped on it and pulled upwards, as if breaking it. A spontaneous roar erupted from the class as the group cupped their ears and marched back to their seats singing "Glory, Glory Hallelujah."

The door opened abruptly and Chelsea sneaked into the classroom and took a seat in the back.

"Excellent," said Jalen adding, "not to forget your papers. Corliss?"

Corliss, decked out in a blue civil war jacket (borrowed from Jalen) led his group to the front of the class. "This report focuses on General Thomas. As an art major, I got side-tracked a bit. Why? The statue of General Thomas and a statue—one of my favorites—called 'The Freedman,' were both sculpted by the same person, John Quincy Adams Ward. Here is a picture of 'The Freedman.' The statue of General Thomas is considered by many to be the finest equestrian statue in Wash., D.C." Corliss altered his voice to project more gruffly and saluted smartly.

"It is an honor and a privilege for me to appear before you today." as he spoke, members of his group executed a soft drum roll, imitating the cadence of soldiers in whispers, marching to "your left, your left, your left, right left."

"My name is George H. Thomas. Probably, very few have heard of me, except of course, those splendid gentlemen whom I got to know at Chickamauga and Nashville. I was greatly honored by the wonderful and vividly expressive statue of myself and my horse, Billy..."

One of the female students in this group donned an extra large set of horse ears and wiggled them as if listening to signs of battle in far off places. "That animal was an astute listener, and I would work with Billy to reinforce my own ears as a battle raged. At Chickamauga, it became more and more apparent that the Rebels were a determined and fearsome foe. Later at Nashville, I was supported at Fort Negley with the tireless efforts of former slaves, some cooks, many teamsters, and of course, the many brave colored troops who fought valiantly at Overton Hill. I did have my doubts about the viability of using black soldiers, but when given the chance, they showed that they were willing to fight and die."

One of this group had a trumpet, and started playing taps, while the others hummed the tune. Two members walked across the stage, one facing forward, the other backward. The first carried a chain, the second a wooden rifle.

"...for freedom; not just for themselves, but also for successive generations of young black men and women.

The class gave this group a big hand, tempered with the recognition that many black soldiers, newly freed slaves, never got to enjoy the freedom for which they fought.

"Marsha?"

Marsha stood up and sang in a beautiful alto voice, "John Brown's Body," to the tune of the Battle Hymn of the Republic.

"I suppose that many of you wonder mightily about why black folk would sing a song dedicated to a white man and that would be quite a valid question, especially given the racial conditions of the time.
There was vivid and crude racism that I witnessed personally during those early years of the fight for abolition—for abolishing slavery. The rebels wanted and fought hard, to extend slavery across the face of the entire nation. Even wanted it in the new states that were coming into the nation and tried to force slavery down our throats in Kansas. And the fugitive slave law was the last straw I think for so many of us who despised the institution. Now, before I was hung..."

Here the entire group started humming 'John Brown's Body,' "I tried to organize an uprising in the slave-holding states, but fell short of my goal. Nobody wants to die before their time, whether by drowning or hanging, and I suppose that one is about as good as the other." Then two members stepped in front of the young man reciting and started waving a long blue flag, twenty-feet in length, in front of the group–as if it were one huge wave.

Another student held the chain around the student-reciter, as if it were the hanging rope. "But I have one last thing that I want you to hear. If you hold one hand to your ear , cup your ear like this , on a cold night in the winter, you can hear those slaves singing way down in Georgia, 'John Brown's Body lies a moulderin in the grave.'"

As the song developed, Devan spoke about the "Incident at Ebenezer Creek." The Georgia slaves that thirsted for freedom cooked, cleaned, cleared trees, and washed clothing to secure food from Union troops as they left behind shackles on the plantations of Georgia. Here is a description of their experience at Ebenezer Creek. The group sank to the floor as a citation was read;

"On December 9, 1864, during the American Civil War, U.S. Gen. Jeff. C. Davis crossed Ebenezer Creek with his 14th Army Corps as it advanced toward Savannah during Gen. William T. Sherman's March to the Sea. Davis hastily removed the pontoon bridges over the creek and hundreds of freed slaves following his army drowned trying to swim the swollen waters to escape pursuing Confederates."

"Very moving—you guys are doing an excellent job and you sing beautifully. Next."

Tofu, head held high and decked in a long, flowing blue robe, marched to the front of the room, followed by Damisi, carrying a conga drum. One of the students stepped outside and rolled in the same large trash can that she had slid into a few weeks ago; they turned it upside down and snuggled it, while Tofu sat on the inverted can as she read. Damisi started humming softly, "Gimme that Ole Time Religion."

"Four score and seven years ago our fathers brought forth on this continent, a new nation, conceived in Liberty, and dedicated to the proposition that all men are created equal." It was obvious that she was nervous, but her voice became stronger, quivered less as she continued. "It is rather for us to be here dedicated to the great task remaining before us—that from these honored dead we take increased devotion."

As she read, Damisi took hold of a large ear seized from the biology lab, an oversized cotton swab, and started to plunge the ear, obviously of wax, which she deposited in an old wax can. The two fellow students took over the rhythm and humming, hanging the chains vertically and using mallets to maintain the sound.

"...that this nation, under God, shall have a new birth of freedom—and that government of the people, by the people, for the people, shall not perish from the earth."

When finished, Tofu took four marshmallows, two on each side, from the insides of her mouth. She and Damisi took bows to thunderous applause. Tofu was anxious to get to her seat, and departed the front of the room, took another bow, and asked, "Now Mr. Harkness, we heard that you had an interesting reenactment at the Crater—what did you learn?"

There were just a few minutes in the period as Jalen inhaled the question, winked at Chelsea, and started, "Folks, there are tons of lessons to be learned from the Civil War—the one I learned this time was to mind my trust; first , how I invest my trust and secondly, that one must assess capacity for trust.

You guys have met the challenge of understanding some of the history in your backyards; somewhere between DuBois and Washington, Malcom and Martin, Ida Wells and Sojourner Truth, lies that place—a place beyond Cemetery Hill, where you plant flowers, nourish your skill for learning. Chelsea, who you guys know as my wife holds the key to my trust in her heart; If it weren't for her, I might not be here today. Those are both lifetime jobs. Another thing that you guys have given me today is an appreciation for those who have worked to achieve justice; thanks for sharing!"

So Jalen, remember your visit to hell, your rendezvous with the Crater fondly. After the war, my Dorsey kinfolk stayed in Baltimore; not me. I needed to be further north in New Jersey, far away from those crab-legged red-necks. Damned near kilt Lincoln when he passed through Baltimore roundabouts '61; didn't want 'em to know where I was. Wasn't safe in Maryland, too much attention. Spoke to Grant about it—Medal of Honor winner in Maryland?—hell no. Harass me, wife too. Safer with no memoirs, no interviews. Now that you done cratered, you might understand what I did—kept my mouth shut, whereabouts real private. As it was, I died from rheumatism; all those damn mosquitoes—effects of malaria. Didn't want my wife ever to suffer on my account. Loved her too much. Being a hero can be a burden, especially if you are in the midst of chaotic evil, and slavery was a great terrorizing, killing evil. I chose NOT to be remembered, preferred privacy. No pictures, no interviews, no memoirs—General Thomas did the same thing, except for the pictures. He couldn't do a damn thing about the statue, God bless his soul. Provincial laws prevented institutions from rescuing the slaves; many of those same institutions half-step to this day with great injury to children. But bless your peaked soul, we still be here talking, chatting—I thought you'd be long gone by now. I still ask myself if Old Pleasants built a tunnel to freedom or a bridge to hell. By the way, hold on to those rosy sun-glasses—they are your gift from President Lincoln.

www.ingramcontent.com/pod-product-compliance
Lightning Source LLC
Chambersburg PA
CBHW060514130626
46553CB00002B/486